THE MOST COMPLETE AND EASY-TO-FOLLOW CALIFORNIA DMV EXAM HANDBOOK WITH 250 PRACTICE QUESTIONS

OUR COMPREHENSIVE, UP-TO-DATE GUIDE WILL
MAKE IT EFFORTLESS TO PASS YOUR PERMIT TEST

DRIVE SAFELY PUBLISHING

CONTENTS

LEGAL DISCLAIMER

The QR codes for the downloadable flashcards and audio files for the practice exams are located on the last page of the book.

This handbook has been created with the utmost care and dedication to providing accurate, helpful, and comprehensive information regarding the rules, regulations, and procedures associated with driving in the state of California.

However, it is crucial to understand that this handbook is intended solely for educational purposes and as a guide to assist individuals in preparing for the California Department of Motor Vehicles (DMV) examination. Please **do not** go directly to the questions and answers at the back of the book. It is of vital importance that you read the material to understand the questions asked on the test since the wording can vary significantly depending on the version of the test you get. This book does not replace or supersede any official publications or regulations provided by the California DMV or any other relevant legal authorities.

The author, instructors, and publishers of this handbook shall not be held responsible or liable for any actions, incidents, accidents, or consequences that may occur as a result of applying the information provided within this book. Driving is an intricate and dynamic activity, and while we strive to offer accurate guidance, we cannot anticipate or control the specific circumstances and decisions made by individual drivers.

Driving comes with great responsibility. It is the driver's sole responsibility to adhere to all applicable laws, regulations, and guidelines provided by the California DMV and other relevant authorities. This handbook should be used in conjunction with official DMV resources and instruction from certified driving instructors.

For specific questions, concerns, or legal advice regarding your driving privileges, it is strongly recommended that you consult with qualified legal professionals or officials from the California DMV.

Please be aware that laws, regulations, and procedures related to driving can change over time. While we strive to keep this handbook as up-to-date as possible, it is essential for readers to verify information with the latest official sources, such as the California DMV's official publications and website.

By using this handbook, you acknowledge and accept the terms of this disclaimer, understanding that you are solely responsible for your actions and decisions while driving in the state of California.

Safe and responsible driving is of paramount importance, and we encourage all readers to prioritize safety, respect traffic laws, and continuously improve their knowledge and skills as responsible drivers.

INTRODUCTION

In the golden haze of a California morning, the road stretched ahead like a promise, a ribbon of asphalt winding through landscapes that ranged from sun-soaked beaches to towering redwood forests. But there, lurking between you and the exhilarating freedom of the open road, stands a formidable gatekeeper: the California DMV exam.

Picture this: You're seated in a nondescript room, clutching a pamphlet that looks more like an encrypted treasure map than a guide to navigating the intricacies of the road. The air is thick with nervous anticipation, the chairs are rigid reminders of the task ahead, and your heart beats a little faster as you glance at the line of fellow aspiring drivers, all on the cusp of embarking on their motoring journeys.

Countless hours of studying traffic laws and memorizing road signs have led to this moment, but you can't shake off the overwhelming anxiety. What if you fail? What if the test is more complicated than you anticipated? No matter your age—whether a teenager or adult learner—one thing is certain: the California DMV exam can feel like an insurmountable peak in your journey. Now, imagine a guide that promises to turn this daunting task into a breeze, a handbook that breaks down the labyrinth of driving rules into manageable, understandable lessons that prepare you for success, the key to unlocking the highway to freedom, confidence, and California sunsets.

As you hold this book, it's evident that you're on a journey, seeking mastery over a seemingly formidable obstacle. Perhaps it's the allure of newfound freedom that propels you forward, the promise of untamed highways and boundless horizons waiting just beyond that driver's license. Maybe you're standing at a crossroads, an unwavering determination simmering within you to conquer the bureaucratic maze and claim your correct place on California's roads. Or it could be that you're a devoted parent, watching with a mixture of trepidation and pride as your child stands on the precipice of driving independence, yearning to equip them with the knowledge and confidence they need.

You see, beyond the title of this book lies a shared understanding—the understanding that this journey is about more than just passing a test. It's about empowerment. It's about the rush of adrenaline as you merge onto the freeway for the first time, the satisfaction of navigating complex intersections flawlessly, and the pride in being a responsible, confident driver. This book isn't just about memorizing rules; it's about gaining the tools to navigate life's pathways with poise.

By embarking on the journey through these pages, you open the door to a realm of benefits that will expedite your path to success on the DMV exam and beyond. Here's a preview of the invaluable shortcuts this book offers:

- **Simplified learning:** The labyrinth of complex driving laws and intricate regulations is meticulously deciphered within these pages. With language that's clear, concise, and easy to comprehend, you'll swiftly grasp fundamental concepts that might have once seemed inscrutable.

- **Effective study guide:** The overwhelming bulk of the official DMV handbook is deftly deconstructed into bite-sized sections that facilitate systematic learning. It's time to say goodbye to the specter of information overload; this book's structured approach streamlines your study process, rendering it far more efficient and manageable.
- **Comprehensive practice questions:** Encompassing an expansive array of practice questions, this book propels you beyond rote memorization. Immerse yourself in exercises that simulate the real DMV test environment, refining your ability to apply acquired knowledge and acquainting you with the exam's format.
- **Real-life driving scenarios:** While the DMV test gauges your theoretical grasp of the law, it's on the road where the knowledge truly comes to life. This book doesn't just prepare you for the test; it equips you for real-world driving scenarios, bridging the gap between theoretical understanding and practical application.
- **Boost confidence:** As the hours of dedicated study accumulate and your grasp of the material solidifies, your confidence will inevitably burgeon. The fear of facing the DMV exam will be supplanted by assurance in your preparedness, minimizing the apprehension that often accompanies high-stakes assessments.
- **Save time:** In the quest for knowledge, time is a precious commodity. Rather than trawling through a multitude of resources, this handbook compiles everything you require in one convenient place. Streamline your efforts, channel your focus, and reclaim the hours you would have otherwise spent sifting through disparate materials.
- **Expert advice:** Beyond the confines of conventional DMV handbooks, the author's wealth of experience in driving instruction shines through. Benefit from insights born of practical teaching, providing you with nuanced perspectives that enrich your understanding of the rules of the road.

- **Future driving success:** Your aspirations reach beyond the boundaries of the DMV exam; they encompass a future of driving responsibility and safety. As you absorb the wisdom within these pages, you're not only preparing to pass a test, but you're also laying the foundation for a lifetime of conscientious driving habits that safeguard not only yourself but also fellow road users.

In essence, this book is more than a study tool; it's a companion, a mentor, and a conduit to your road-ready triumph. So, seize the opportunity, embrace the shortcuts, and embark on a journey that transcends exams, fostering a safer, more informed future behind the wheel.

Get ready to fasten your seatbelt as we embark on this adventure together. From the basics to the nuances, from the seemingly straight-forward to the trickiest of scenarios, this handbook is meticulously crafted to be your ultimate companion. By the time you turn the final page, you'll not only be armed with the knowledge to pass the DMV exam with flying colors but also equipped with the confidence to navigate the roads like a true aficionado.

Get ready to head out on the open road toward the California dream —one road sign at a time, one intersection at a time. The journey starts now, and the destination is clear: your license to explore the breathtaking views and vibrant tapestry of the Golden State.

Together, let's demystify the DMV's labyrinthine corridors, decode its enigmatic signs, and embrace the confidence that arises from under-standing. Through this book, you're not just preparing for an exam— you're forging your passage toward a brighter, more capable future on California's roads.

As you embark on the enlightening ride through the pages of this handbook, a transformative end result awaits you, one that extends far beyond the confines of a mere driver's exam. By immersing your-self in this comprehensive guide, you're on the cusp of achieving not only the coveted DMV license but also an elevated understanding of the road, a heightened sense of confidence, and a future filled with safer, more responsible driving.

Picture yourself confidently gliding through the DMV exam, the once-arduous questions unraveling effortlessly before you. Feel the weight of nervous anticipation replaced with the thrill of assured knowledge. Envision yourself navigating the roads of California with a newfound sense of mastery, effortlessly interpreting road signs, adhering to right-of-way protocols, and maneuvering complex intersections with an ease you once deemed unattainable.

But what makes the author the proper authority, the best person to guide you on this journey? The answer lies in their extensive experience and unparalleled expertise in the realm of driving instruction. Having spent over a decade educating aspiring drivers and diligently studying the nuances of California's driving laws, the author stands as a beacon of wisdom and a trusted mentor.

Consider the challenging landscape that existed before the advent of this "new" information—a landscape where the DMV exam was a formidable hurdle, and deciphering the intricacies of California's driving laws was akin to unlocking a cryptic code. The scarcity of accessible resources often led to feelings of frustration, uncertainty, and even repeated exam failures. Many brave souls stumbled through the test, grappling with convoluted content and vague explanations.

Now, envision the transformation. With this book in hand, you're equipped with a roadmap that guides you through every twist and turn of the DMV exam. This guide bridges the gap between inexperience and mastery, unraveling complex topics into digestible segments and presenting real-life scenarios that illuminate the practical application of each rule of the road.

In a landscape where misinformation abounds and anxiety often takes the driver's seat, *The Most Complete and Easy-to-Follow California DMV Exam Handbook With 250 Practice Questions* emerges as the beacon of clarity you've been seeking. Feel the assurance that comes from having the correct information at your fingertips from the tutelage of an experienced guide who understands your journey intimately.

As you stand at this crossroads, eager to seize the wheel of your driving destiny, allow yourself to embrace the certainty that this is not just any book—this is the right book for you. With every turn of the page, you're stepping onto the expressway toward success, confidence, and a future defined by skilled, responsible driving.

1

UNDERSTANDING THE LICENSING PROCESSING SYSTEM

D id you know California has over 26 million licensed drivers, and thousands of new teenagers join this group every year? Here's how they do it.

Becoming a licensed driver in California is a significant milestone, signifying your journey to freedom and independence. This chapter covers the steps and requirements for obtaining a California driver's license, from your visit to the DMV to the day you get your new license.

As you continue reading, you'll discover valuable information about driving, the rules of the road, and your responsibilities as a licensed driver. It's essential to remember that having a driver's license is a privilege that can be revoked. To maintain your driver's license, you must be a responsible and safe driver.

So, get ready for this adventure. Let's explore the steps and prepare you to join the ranks of California's proud and skilled licensed drivers.

Please note the California DMV now has an online process to do the knowledge test at home, create a "my DMV account" and follow the prompts on the DMV website. Upon successfully passing the exam, you will then go to the DMV to present the required paperwork and get the official permit print out.

The California Department of Motor Vehicles establishes the age requirement for minors, 15 ½ years old, to be eligible to apply for a learner's permit. The learner's permit is the stepping stone to gaining practical experience behind the wheel. This permit allows the student driver to practice driving while supervised by a licensed driver at least 25 years old.

The DMV chooses 15 ½ as the minimum age to strike a balance between allowing young individuals to start learning how to drive while ensuring they have reached a level of maturity that promotes responsible and safe driving practices. At 15 ½, you've likely gained a basic understanding of traffic rules and road etiquette through theo-retical education; as you progress in your teenage years, you'll be better equipped to comprehend the intricacies of driving regulations and make well-informed decisions on the road.

Before you arrive at the DMV to apply for your learner's permit, it is best that you have the correct documents in your possession. These documents serve as your identification and validation.

The DMV requires proof of identity, and the following documents are acceptable: a valid U.S. passport, a certified birth certificate, a Perma-nent Resident Card (Green Card), or a Consular Report of Birth Abroad.

The DMV requires proof of validity of your social security number (SSN), and the following documents are acceptable: Your Social Secu-rity card, a W-2 form, or a pay stub that bears your whole SSN.

The DMV requires proof of residency in California, and the following documents are acceptable: A utility bill, rental or lease agreement, bank statement, or mortgage statement.

Minors applying for a Learner's permit must provide proof of completing a driver's education course. Certified driving schools provide the driver's education course, and depending on the school, it can be completed either online or in person. Upon completing the driver's education course, the driving school issues a completion certificate to the student.

The DMV process can be cumbersome, so having the correct forms for your visit to the California Department of Motor Vehicles is essential. Choose the appropriate driver's license application: class 'C' for regular passenger vehicles, class 'A' or 'B' for commercial driver's license applicants, and minors must provide the parental consent form.

Take your time and prioritize accuracy and thoroughness; fill out all required fields. Prioritize clear and concise handwriting. Each character should be easily readable. Remember that the information you provide on the form will be used for processing your application, making legibility a crucial factor.

Missing or incomplete information can delay or even cause the driver's license application to be rejected. Double-check details like your name, date of birth, Social Security number, and other particulars. Even minor discrepancies can lead to complications during the application process.

Certain sections of the form may require supporting documents or identification numbers. Follow instructions carefully and attach copies of necessary documents if requested. Providing accurate information ensures smooth verification and processing.

Be sure to take a moment to read and understand the specific instructions for each section, as it ensures that you provide information in the correct format and adhere to any additional requirements.

Before submitting the forms, verify that you have signed and dated all the required spaces; take a moment to conduct a thorough review and double-check the information you've provided with your supporting documents. This meticulous review ensures the accuracy and completeness of your application. If any section of the form presents uncertainty, seek assistance, refer to the DMV website (dmv.ca.gov), or consult with someone knowledgeable about this process.

Be sure to account for and be prepared for all application fees and payment methods acceptable to the DMV.

It is recommended that you make an appointment with the DMV to ease the process and avoid a long wait time. The DMV has embraced technological advancements to simplify the process of making appointments. The Online Appointment System is your gateway to securing a time slot that aligns with your availability. This system revolutionizes the way you interact with the DMV, transforming what used to be a waiting game into an efficient and organized experience.

Begin by accessing the official California DMV website (dmv.ca.gov), but before you begin the appointment scheduling process, gather all the essential information you'll need to provide, such as your identification number, Social Security number, any other forms for acceptable identification, and any other specific details related to your appointment category. Being prepared with this information will make the scheduling process smoother and quicker. Note that to do transactions online on the DMV website, you must create a "My DMV Account."

Go to the Online Appointment System, select your appointment category, follow the prompts to provide required information, and choose a convenient time slot to align your DMV visit with your schedule.

Upon selecting your appointment time, save the confirmation number provided by the system as proof of your appointment, either by noting it down or digitally. This confirmation serves as a tangible reference for your DMV visit.

Arrive at the DMV early to avoid delays and avoid scheduling commitments too soon after your appointment to reduce potential stress.

A DMV representative will review and verify your documents, ensuring everything is in order before proceeding.

If you're applying for your driver's license for the first time, you will be required to take the written knowledge test. Be confident that you will do well; you will be prepared, as the practice questions in this book will make the test easy.

You will be required to take a picture; this snapshot will become your driver's license image. Additionally, fingerprinting is a standard procedure to confirm your identity.

Now that you understand the documentation and DMV appointment process, you're ready to confidently proceed. While paperwork may seem complex, it's crucial for getting your California driver's license. There are more steps ahead, but each one takes you closer to your goal. Gather your documents, complete the forms, book your DMV appointment, and stay motivated. The destination—your California driver's license—is within reach.

THE WRITTEN EXAM

The written exam comprehensively evaluates your knowledge of traffic rules, road signs, and safe driving practices. It's a pivotal step in ensuring you possess the information necessary to navigate the roads safely and responsibly.

Read, take notes, and make sure you truly understand it. But don't stop there. You've got a bank of practice test questions in this book and online at the DMV website (dmv.ca.gov). These practice rounds aren't just warm-ups. They're a chance for you to size up your knowledge and get familiar with how the actual exam will look. Taking these practice tests isn't just about knowing the material but mastering your "how-to" for the exam.

Remember, this phase is about the basics of responsible driving. Nail down those road signs, traffic rules, and safe driving habits—that's where it all begins.

Now, here's a trick: Visualize your success. Picture yourself confidently and correctly answering those questions during the exam. This mental prep can knock out anxiety and prepare you to roll.

Speaking of questions, here's what you'll face: Multiple-choice questions. Each question gives you a situation or a question, and you have a set of answers. Your job is simple: Pick the correct answer according to the driving laws and what makes sense on the road.

This book covers virtually everything the exam includes—from who gets the right-of-way to speed limits, recognizing road signs, and understanding their meanings. One of the purposes of the exam is to test how well you know the basics of driving.

Be sure to take your time to read the questions carefully, think them through, and pick your answer within the time limit. Remember, you need a passing score of 83% or better, you must get at least 38 of the 46 questions correct. If you fail the knowledge test three times, you must start the application process again and pay a new fee.

Keep in mind this isn't just about passing a test. It's about getting equipped with the know-how to make solid choices on the road. Let's get down to business and ensure you're all set to drive responsibly and confidently in California.

THE VISION EXAM

The vision exam evaluates your ability to perceive and respond to visual cues while operating a vehicle. Here's an overview of what this exam entails, according to the Department of Motor Vehicles in California (DMV) (n.d.):

- **Visual acuity assessment:** This part of the exam focuses on your ability to see things crisply at different distances. You'll usually read off a set of letters or numbers from a chart. This skill ensures you're capable of spotting road signs, signals, and potential trouble from a good distance away.
- **Peripheral vision evaluation:** Your peripheral vision, or what you can see at the edges of your sight, is a big deal since it's super important for detecting any surprises or dangers lurking on the sides while you're driving.
- **Color perception testing:** This part of the exam is all about making sure you can tell those colors apart accurately. It's like ensuring you're not mistaking a red light for a green one.

According to the DMV (n.d.), your vision should meet or exceed 20/40 when both eyes are considered, this means you should have the same visual acuity at 20 feet as a person with normal vision has at 40 feet, whether or not you use corrective lenses. If you fail the initial screening, the protocol is to refer you to a vision specialist. This professional will comprehensively examine your vision and then complete the Report of Vision Examination (DL 62) form. The goal is to ensure that your visual capacity aligns with the demands of safe driving.

Unlike the written exam, the vision exam doesn't follow a pass/fail scoring system. Instead, it evaluates whether your visual acuity and peripheral vision meet the minimum requirements for safe driving, ensuring you possess the necessary capabilities to navigate the roads responsibly.

Now that you have learned about the exams, it's time to talk about the next phase, which is to practice for the behind-the-wheel exam. For all minors, the DMV has a mandatory wait time of 6 months from the issue date of attaining the learner's permit before they are eligible to take the behind-the-wheel test. All minors must attain a 6-hour completion certificate from a certified driving school. Additionally, all minors are to practice an additional 50 hours (not including the 6 hours with the driving school), with 10 being at night. Be sure to log all the practice hours, a handy log is available at the back of the book. For minors, a driving school instructor will sign the learner's permit upon finalizing the first driving lesson, making it valid for the minor to practice with any licensed driver 25 years or older seated in the front passenger seat. None of the mandated driving hour requirements or completion certificate with a driving school is required for any applicant 18 or older; they are encouraged to get as much practice as possible to gain mastery of their driving before making an appointment for the behind-the-wheel test. Note that the permit is only valid to practice with a licensed driver who is at least 25 for both minors and adults, the difference being that a Driving School doesn't need to sign the learner's permit to validate it for any student learner that is 17 ½ and older.

It is best to practice with someone who has extensive driving experience, patience, and the ability to offer constructive feedback. The hours spent together should be characterized by mentorship and guidance, as these aspects significantly shape your driving proficiency.

The role of the adult supervisor extends beyond the fulfillment of hours; it is a role of mentorship, guidance, and instilling the essence of responsible driving behavior.

YOUR PROGRESS CHECKLIST

To help you track your progress to getting your learner's permit and ensure that no step is missed, we've created a comprehensive checklist. Keep this checklist handy and mark each milestone as you achieve it. Let's embark on this journey of preparation and progress together.

Driver Education and Training

[ ] Completed a state-approved driver education program.

Written Test Preparation

[ ] Thoroughly studied the California Driver Handbook.

[ ] Have developed an understanding of road signs, traffic rules, and safe driving practices.

[ ] Utilized the practice questions in this book and on the DMV website to assess your knowledge and readiness.

Documentation Collection

[ ] Gathered proof of identity, Social Security number and California residency.

[ ] Collected required documentation and supporting materials.

Form Completion

[ ] Filled out the Driver's License or Identification Card Application (DL 44 or DL 44C) form accurately and completely.

Appointment Scheduling

[ ] Scheduled a DMV appointment.

Final Preparations

[ ] Double-checked all required documents and paperwork.

[ ] Arranged necessary identification for the DMV visit.

[ ] Ensured familiarity with the DMV location and directions.

DMV Appointment

[ ] Attended the scheduled DMV appointment.

[ ] Presented all required documents and identification.

[ ] Successfully completed any necessary tests or evaluations.

Written Test Success

[ ] Passed the written test.

[ ] Secured a learner's permit.

Behind-The-Wheel Training

[ ] Continued practicing driving skills with the guidance of a licensed driver 25 or older.

[ ] Developed confidence in various driving scenarios, such as city driving, highway navigation, and parking.

Professional Driving Lessons

[ ] Attained a 6-hour completion certificate from a certified Driving School.

Driving Test Preparation

[ ] Developed practical skills for maneuvering the vehicle.

[ ] Gained an understanding of road etiquette and safe driving behavior.

[ ] Practiced parallel parking, three-point turns, and other essential maneuvers.

Driving Test Success

[ ] Passed the driving test.

Obtaining Your Driver's License (Provisional for Minors)

[ ] Received your driver's license.

As you progress through each phase of the licensing process, use this checklist to keep track of your achievements. This roadmap serves as a visual representation of your progress and a motivational tool, guiding you toward successfully acquiring your California driver's license. Each tick mark represents a step closer to your goal—the day you confidently take the wheel and embrace the privileges and responsibilities of a licensed driver. Stay focused, diligent, and on track as you journey toward this exciting new chapter of your life. Now that you're familiar with the steps required to get your driver's license, let's dive into the first big hurdle: understanding California's traffic laws.

2

EXPLORING CALIFORNIA TRAFFIC LAWS

A s you begin your journey to becoming a confident and knowledgeable driver, you must thoroughly understand the rules that govern our roadways. From the majestic coastline to the towering redwoods, California offers a majestic backdrop for your driving adventures. However, even in the Golden State, some "free" things can come with a price tag. Case in point: Have you ever wondered why a California driver received a traffic citation at a supposedly free parking lot? The answer lies in the realm of traffic laws.

While you navigate through this comprehensive handbook, you'll gain an in-depth understanding of the regulations that keep our roads safe, the consequences of not following them, and strategies to help you avoid costly pitfalls.

With its diverse landscapes and bustling cities, California presents an array of driving scenarios that require a keen grasp of traffic laws. Each region has unique challenges, from the congested streets of Los Angeles to the serene highways of the Central Valley. It's crucial to approach your driving experience armed with knowledge that helps you navigate confidently and safeguards you from unintended infractions.

In addition to covering essential driving laws and regulations, we will cover lesser-known ones that could catch even the most experienced drivers off-guard. We'll discuss everything from right-of-way rules to specific speed limits, parking intricacies, and the proper use of turn signals, to name a few. By the time you finish this chapter, you'll have a comprehensive understanding of the rules that contribute to the orderly flow of traffic in California.

Since laws are constantly updated, it's vital to stay up-to-date. Here, we'll guide you on how to keep track of any modifications or additions to the existing regulations. Being informed about changes ensures you're always driving within the legal boundaries and minimizing the risk of fines, penalties, or even more severe consequences.

Whether you're a new or experienced driver, this chapter is your go-to resource for mastering California's traffic laws. A good grasp of these rules ensures a safer and more enjoyable driving experience. Let's begin this journey through California's traffic laws.

IN-DEPTH REVIEW OF THE TRAFFIC LAWS

Basic Road Rules

It's important to know the core principles of California's traffic laws. A firm understanding of these principles is essential for safe and responsible driving. Here, we will explore topics that encompass speed limits, right of way, yielding, stopping, and turning rules, among others.

Speed Limits

Speed limits in California serve as a safeguard for all road users. These limits fluctuate, accommodating for things like the type of road, surrounding environment, and weather conditions. Adhering to posted speed limits is paramount, as excessive speed can result in accidents and traffic violations. Here are the key takeaways:

- Upon entering every road, look for and follow all the posted speed limits. These limits are meticulously determined based on road design, traffic volume, and nearby establishments.
- The California Basic Speed Law mandates drivers adjust their speed based on driving conditions, irrespective of the posted speed limit, meaning drivers must reduce their speed to what is safe and prudent in adverse weather, heavy traffic, or hazardous situations.

Right-Of-Way

Understanding and respecting right-of-way regulations is essential to smooth traffic flow and prevent collisions. Some things to keep in mind:

- At all-way-stop intersections (every approaching corner has a stop sign), the vehicle that arrives first is granted the right of way. If two vehicles reach the intersection simultaneously, the vehicle on the right takes precedence.
- A green light at an intersection signifies your right to proceed. However, it is crucial to yield to pedestrians or vehicles that are still in the intersection.
- A yellow light means the intersection is transitioning from a green light to a red light. You, as a driver, must determine if a safe stop can still be made or to continue through the intersection; it is not against the law to enter the intersection while the traffic light remains yellow; it is against the law to enter once the traffic light is red.

- A red light means to make a complete stop.

Yielding

Yielding involves granting precedence to other road users before proceeding. This practice is integral to averting accidents and maintaining an orderly traffic flow. Key yielding rules include:

- Upon encountering a yield sign, decelerate and be prepared to stop for pedestrians and vehicles with the right-of-way.
- Pedestrians are to be granted the right of way in both designated and unmarked crosswalks. It is incumbent upon you to stop and allow them to finish crossing safely.

Stops

Making complete stops is not only the law but also greatly improves safety. A complete stop encompasses the vehicle coming to a full motionless position, being behind the limit line, and the driver looking left, right, and left again to confirm it is safe to proceed.

Vital stopping rules encompass:

- Bring your vehicle to a complete stop when approaching a school bus that has flashing red lights and a stop signal arm displayed.
- Whenever you approach a school bus displaying flashing red lights and an extended stop sign, all vehicles must come to a stop, regardless of their direction of travel. Except for vehicles on the opposite side of a multi-lane road or when there is a dividing wall on single-lane roads, in which case only the lanes traveling in the direction of the school bus need to stop.

Turning Rules

Making turns in a safe and controlled manner is crucial for the safety of all drivers. Remember the following regarding making turns:

- Provided that there is no sign prohibiting it, you are allowed to make a right turn on a red light after coming to a complete stop and yielding to pedestrians and oncoming traffic.
- When making a left turn, give way to oncoming traffic and pedestrians, and proceed only when it's safe.
- There are protected left turns, meaning you have a green arrow that stops every other driver who could interfere with you as they see a red light on their side of the street. There are "unprotected" left turns; in these turns, the driver gets a green light without an arrow; the opposite side of traffic gets the same green as you, oncoming traffic, and pedestrians have the right-of-way over the driver making the left turn. It's important to remember that responsible and courteous driving is not just a legal obligation but also a shared duty for all individuals utilizing the roadways.

PARKING LAWS

A comprehensive grasp of these rules is vital to avoid penalties, maintain traffic flow, and respect the needs of all road users.

Colored Curb Meanings

Colored curbs are strategically employed to convey specific parking restrictions and permissions. Understanding what these curb colors mean is crucial to avoiding parking violations and inconveniences. Here's what you need to know:

- **Red curbs:** Parking is strictly forbidden at red curbs at all times. These zones are reserved for emergency vehicles exclusively, ensuring swift response during emergencies.

- **Yellow curbs:** Yellow curbs indicate loading or unloading zones. Vehicles can briefly stop here to load or unload passengers or goods, with the driver required to stay with the vehicle.
- **Green curbs:** Green curbs allow parking for a limited time; signage typically indicates the time limits drivers must adhere to.
- **White curbs:** A white curb indicates that parking is allowed for picking up or dropping off passengers.
- **Blue curbs:** Blue curbs indicate parking reserved for individuals with disabilities. These reserved parking spaces play a crucial role in enabling individuals with disabilities to access facilities and services.

Honoring these spaces isn't just a legal obligation but also a reflection of empathy. Here's what you should be aware of:

- **Fines and consequences:** Illegally parking in a handicapped space can result in substantial fines and the potential for your vehicle to get towed.

Street Cleaning Regulations

Street cleaning is crucial for upholding the cleanliness and appearance of the city's streets. Familiarizing yourself with street cleaning schedules and restrictions is essential to avoid citations or having your vehicle towed. Consider the following:

- **Posted signs:** Pay careful attention to posted signs indicating street cleaning days and times. Parking during these hours can lead to fines or towing.
- **Street sweeper signs:** In certain areas, street cleaning occurs on alternating sides of the street on different days. Ensure you know which side to park on to avoid penalties.

Parking regulations are vital to preserving order on California's roads and ensuring equitable access for all road users.

Adhering to these parking laws actively contributes to a more organized and considerate driving environment.

DRIVING UNDER THE INFLUENCE (DUI) LAWS

Learning these laws is essential for maintaining road safety and preventing potentially dangerous situations. We will outline the blood alcohol concentration (BAC) limits and the corresponding penalties associated with DUI offenses in California.

Blood Alcohol Concentration Limits

According to Ramos (n.d): "Blood alcohol concentration (BAC) is a measure of the amount of alcohol present in a person's bloodstream". In California, the legal BAC limit for most drivers is

- **0.08% BAC:** It is illegal for individuals 21 years of age and older to have a BAC of 0.08% or greater and operate a motor vehicle.

For certain groups, stricter BAC limits apply:

- **0.04% BAC:** Commercial drivers operating commercial vehicles are subject to a lower BAC limit of 0.04%.
- **0.01% BAC:** Drivers under the age of 21 are prohibited from operating a motor vehicle with any measurable amount of alcohol in their system; this is commonly referenced as "zero tolerance."

Penalties for DUI Offenses

Operating a motor vehicle in California under the influence of alcohol or drugs is against the law, and the penalties reflect the gravity of the situation. The penalties for DUI offenses can vary based on factors such as prior DUI convictions and the circumstances of the offense. Here is an overview of the potential penalties for DUI offenses:

- **First DUI offense:** Penalties for a first-time DUI offense may include fines, license suspension, mandatory attendance at DUI school, and possible jail time or probation. Additionally, it might be required for individuals caught driving under the influence that they install an ignition interlock device (breathalyzer) in their vehicle.
- **Subsequent DUI offenses:** Penalties escalate for repeat offenses. Subsequent DUI convictions can lead to extended license suspension periods, higher fines, and possibly jail time.
- **Aggravated DUI:** If the DUI offense involves factors such as excessive BAC, causing injury or death, or driving with a driver's license that is suspended, the penalties can be significantly more severe. Aggravated DUI offenses may result in extended jail time, longer license suspension, and potential felony charges.
- **DUI causing injury or death:** If a DUI results in injury or death to another person, the penalties can include substantial fines, lengthy prison sentences, and permanent revocation of driving privileges.

Understanding California's DUI laws and the associated penalties is crucial for maintaining road safety and making responsible decisions while operating a motor vehicle. Adhering to the legal BAC limits and avoiding impaired driving safeguards your well-being and protects all road users' safety. It's essential to remember that DUI offenses can have far-reaching consequences, underscoring the importance of making informed and responsible choices behind the wheel.

IMPLICATIONS OF VIOLATING THESE LAWS

Penalties for Traffic Rule Violations

Understanding these penalties is vital for promoting responsible driving behavior, ensuring road safety, and preventing potential legal consequences. We will provide an in-depth account of the penalties that may follow various traffic rule violations, including fines, points, license suspension, and imprisonment.

Types of Consequences for Traffic Violations

Fines

Fines are a common penalty for traffic violations in California. The fine amount can vary depending on which traffic offenses are committed. Some traffic violations, such as going over the speed limit or not making complete stops, typically have predetermined fines with additional fees added by the cities and counties where the violation occurred, while others might be determined by a judge based on the circumstances. It's essential to remember that these fines can accumulate if you're repeatedly found in violation of traffic rules.

Points on Driving Record

The California Department of Motor Vehicles (DMV) operates a point system to track driving infractions (DMV, n.d.). Each traffic violation is assessed as a point value, and these are added to your driving record. Getting an excessive number of points from traffic violations within a specific timeframe can lead to substantial ramifications, such as increased insurance premiums, driver's license suspension, and mandatory attendance at a traffic violator school. Four points within a 12-month period, six points within a 24-month period, and eight points within a 36-month period will result in the suspension of the driver's license.

License Suspension or Revocation

Some traffic offenses can lead to temporary or even permanent license suspension or revocation. The severity of the offense and any prior violations on your record will influence the duration of the suspension. Common reasons for license suspension include

- driving under the influence (DUI)
- reckless driving
- excessive speeding
- accumulating too many points on your record within a specific period
- criminal charges

Certain serious traffic violations can result in imprisonment as a penalty. For instance, driving under the influence, fleeing the scene of an accident, road rage, or engaging in street racing can lead to incarceration. The length of imprisonment depends on the nature of the offense and whether it is a repeat offense.

Probation and Mandatory Programs

In some cases, individuals found guilty of traffic violations might be placed on probation. This often comes with specific conditions, such as attending traffic violator school or completing a defensive driving course. These programs aim to educate drivers about safe driving practices and reduce the likelihood of future violations.

Traffic laws must be obeyed to avoid fines, points on your driving record, driver's license suspension, imprisonment, and various other consequences. By following these laws, you protect your safety and contribute to the well-being of fellow road users. It's essential to remember that the enforcement of these penalties aims to foster a safer driving environment for everyone on the road.

According to the DMV website (n.d.), California law categorizes traffic violations into three main types: infractions, misdemeanors, and felonies. Let's explore each category in detail.

INFRACTION—MINOR VIOLATIONS

Infractions are the most common type of traffic violations and are considered minor offenses under California law. These violations often result in fines and are typically less severe than the other two categories. Examples of infractions include

- **Speeding:** Exceeding the posted speed limit.
- **Not stopping at a red light or stop sign:** Disobeying traffic signals.
- **Not making full stops:** Slowing down, but not completely coming to a stop.
- **Not following a sign direction:** Turning right when there is a "no right turn on red sign."
- **Illegal U-Turn:** Making an illegal U-turn where prohibited.
- **Seat belt violation:** Not wearing a seatbelt while driving.
- **Expired registration:** Driving a vehicle with expired registration.
- **Parking violations:** Illegally parking in designated no-parking zones.

Infractions usually carry monetary penalties that vary based on the specific violation. While these violations may not lead to criminal records, they should not be taken lightly, as they contribute to unsafe road conditions and can escalate in fines or consequences against your driver's license if not corrected.

MISDEMEANOR—SERIOUS VIOLATIONS

Misdemeanors are more serious traffic violations that could result in criminal charges. These offenses often involve a higher degree of risk to public safety. Examples of these include:

- **Reckless driving:** Demonstrating a complete disregard for the safety of others while driving a motorized vehicle.
- **Driving under the influence (DUI):** Operating a motorized vehicle while impaired by alcohol or drugs.
- **Hit and run:** Being involved in a collision and leaving the scene without exchanging necessary information or rendering aid.
- **Driving with a suspended license:** Operating a motorized vehicle despite having a suspended or revoked driver's license.
- **Evading a police officer:** Fleeing from law enforcement in a vehicle.

Consequences for misdemeanors can be fines, probation, community service, and even imprisonment. A conviction for a misdemeanor traffic violation can also result in a criminal record that may affect your current job, future employment opportunities, and other aspects of your life.

FELONY—MAJOR VIOLATIONS

Felony traffic violations are the most severe offenses and carry significant legal consequences due to the substantial risk they pose to public safety. Examples of felony traffic violations include

- **Vehicular manslaughter:** Causing the death of another person while operating a vehicle recklessly or under the influence.
- **Repeat DUI offenses:** Multiple convictions for driving under the influence within a certain time frame.

- **Leaving the scene of a fatal accident:** Fleeing the scene of an accident in which a death occurred.
- **Assault with a vehicle:** Using a vehicle as a weapon to harm someone intentionally.

Felony convictions can lead to substantial fines, lengthy prison sentences, and the permanent revocation of driving privileges. The legal and personal consequences of felony traffic violations are severe and far-reaching.

Understanding the categories of traffic violations is essential for all drivers to uphold safety and accountability on California's roads. Whether it's an infraction, a misdemeanor, or a felony, it is every driver's responsibility to adhere to the rules of the road and prioritize the well-being of all those sharing the road with them. By familiarizing ourselves with these distinctions, we create a safer and more orderly driving environment for everyone.

Staying up to date with traffic regulations helps ensure that you always comply with the law and, most importantly, drive safely with others on the road.

HOW TO STAY INFORMED ABOUT CHANGES IN LAWS

The DMV Website (dmv.ca.gov): Your Trustworthy Guide

The California DMV website is an invaluable resource hub for all matters related to driving regulations, road safety, and legal requirements. It's highly recommended that you regularly visit this website to stay informed about any modifications to traffic laws. The DMV website is the official platform for disseminating accurate and up-to-date information about traffic laws in California. The state's authorities maintain it and it is your most reliable source for understanding the latest legal requirements. Any amendments or additions to existing traffic laws are promptly updated on the DMV website so you can quickly access and understand the changes that may affect your driving habits. Navigating through the site to find specific information or updates is straightforward, even for those who might not be tech-savvy.

Local News: Your Window to Community Changes

Local news outlets, whether through newspapers, television, radio, or online platforms, play a crucial role in keeping communities informed about various matters, including updates to traffic laws. These outlets are attuned to the pulse of the region, often covering topics that directly affect residents.

Local news organizations include updates on new traffic signs, speed limit adjustments, and road closures, to name a few. These updates inform the public about changes in driving laws that might affect their daily commutes and overall driving experience.

EXPLORING CALIFORNIA TRAFFIC LAWS—SELF-ASSESSMENT QUIZ

Test your understanding of California traffic laws with the following multiple-choice and true/false questions based on the laws discussed in this chapter. Choose the best answer for each question.

Multiple Choice

1. Which of the following is considered illegal while driving in California?

a) Having a conversation while holding a cell phone in your hand.
b) Using hands-free devices.
c) Using one finger to swipe open your cell phone screen.
d) Making an emergency call.

2. When is it acceptable to make a U-turn in a residential district?

    a) In front of a fire station.

    b) On a curve in the road.

    c) After you have a good view of oncoming traffic.

    d) After ensuring no vehicles are approaching within 200 feet.

3. Drivers shall _____ for an emergency vehicle with its flashing lights:

    a) Slow down and drive carefully around pedestrians.

    b) Pull over and stop.

    c) Change lanes immediately if you are driving in the same lane
    as the emergency vehicle.

    d) Go faster.

4. Drivers are to do the following when approaching a school bus with flashing red lights on their side of the road:

    a) Pass it cautiously.

    b) Stop and proceed once the lights stop flashing.

    c) Slow down and proceed with caution.

    d) Honk to alert the children.

True/False

5. True or False: In California, it is legal to make a right turn on a red arrow after coming to a complete stop unless posted otherwise.

6. True or False: It is legal to leave a child under the age of 6 unattended in a vehicle if the weather is mild.

7. True or False: Drivers are not allowed to wear earplugs or headsets in both ears while driving, except for hearing aids.

8. True or False: When driving on a multilane road in California, slower vehicles should use the rightmost lane, and faster vehicles should use the leftmost lane.

Answers
Multiple Choice
a)   d)   b)   b)
True/False
F   F   T   T

3

COMMON SENSE RULES OF THE ROAD

The way I drive, the way I handle a car, is an expression of my inner feelings.

— LEWIS HAMILTON

California's diverse and dynamic roadways demand more than just adherence to regulations; they require a nuanced understanding of the unspoken language of traffic flow. In these pages, we'll uncover the unwritten rules facilitating interaction between vehicles, pedestrians, and cyclists. More than memorizing right-of-way scenarios, we'll explore the essence of yielding and the significance of maintaining a safety cushion of space for unforeseen situations.

Etiquette is more than a mere formality; it's a way of thinking and behaving that can transform congestion into cohesiveness. Here, you'll discover how simply acknowledging a fellow driver's courtesy can set off a chain reaction of politeness. You'll learn the power of patience in heavy traffic and the generosity of allowing others to merge during peak hours.

This chapter is about embracing the responsibility that comes with being behind the wheel and realizing that your choices influence your safety and those around you.

So, as you delve into the following sections, approach them with an open mind, a readiness to absorb, and a willingness to incorporate these lessons into your driving philosophy. By grasping the fundamental principles of common sense and etiquette on California roads, you're not just preparing for the DMV exam—you're elevating yourself to a higher standard of driver conduct. Let's begin this enlightening journey toward becoming a proficient, respectful, and all-around exceptional driver on the vibrant roads of California.

ESSENTIAL ETIQUETTE FOR CALIFORNIA DRIVERS

Understanding Lane Purpose

As you traverse California's highways and byways, it's imperative to comprehend the speed of drivers according to the lane they travel in. The right lane, often referred to as the "slow lane," plays a pivotal role in orderly traffic movement. It's not a misnomer; the rightmost lane is ideally intended for vehicles traveling at a moderate pace, especially when compared to the left lanes, with the leftmost lane commonly referred to as the "fast lane."

The Overtaking Rule

One of the critical discipline elements of driving in the right lane revolves around overtaking slower-moving vehicles. While the right lane is designed for steady cruising, it's essential to understand that steady traffic flow is critical for safety; therefore, if you find yourself behind a slower vehicle, rather than pressuring the driver into going faster, execute a passing maneuver as safely as possible by going into the left lane and returning to the right lane as soon as it's safely possible to maintain the natural flow of traffic.

Enhancing Traffic Flow

The flow of traffic functions best when vehicles adhere to their respective lanes. By slower vehicles sticking to the rightmost lane, it allows faster-moving traffic to flow smoothly, preventing unnecessary congestion and reducing the chances of abrupt lane changes.

Safety First

Proper lane discipline is about safety. The right lane often accommodates exits, entrance ramps, and merging traffic. Staying in this lane when not overtaking ensures that you're best positioned to handle these situations with minimal disruption to the traffic flow. Additionally, it provides a buffer for vehicles entering the highway, reducing the risk of collisions.

Exceptions and Flexibility

Of course, every rule comes with exceptions. You might be in the right lane for longer durations in certain circumstances due to heavy traffic or road conditions. While it's essential to prioritize traffic flow, safety should remain your foremost concern. Suppose you're consistently passing vehicles and maintaining a faster pace. In that case, temporarily moving to the left lane might be more appropriate. Additionally, it's the law that on single lane highways, if you are driving slower than everyone else, you must pull over to the right as soon as it's safely possible to ease the congestion that has built behind you.

Courtesy to Pedestrians—Respecting the Right-Of-Way

It's essential to remember that drivers share the road with other drivers, motorcyclists, bicyclists, and, most importantly, pedestrians, who have the least protection if involved in a traffic collision.

Pedestrians and Their Priority

Pedestrians are the most vulnerable participants in the traffic equation; therefore, drivers are to give pedestrians the right-of-way at crosswalks or intersections. Additionally, drivers must do their best to stop and give the right-of-way if a pedestrian crosses into other unexpected areas, such as mid-block. As a driver, you have a legal and ethical obligation to yield to pedestrians in these scenarios. Embracing this rule promotes road safety and contributes to a more considerate and harmonious driving culture.

Vigilance at Crosswalks

Marked crosswalks are visual cues for drivers to anticipate pedestrian activity; drivers must maintain a vigilant mindset when approaching a crosswalk—whether at an intersection or a mid-block location. Be prepared to yield to any pedestrians waiting to cross or already on the crosswalk. This practice not only upholds the law but also safeguards the well-being of those on foot.

Intersection Etiquette

Intersections are common areas where vehicular and pedestrian paths intersect. In the realm of pedestrian safety, intersections require heightened attention. When making turns, especially right turns, ensure that your path is clear of pedestrians crossing or about to cross. Remember, pedestrians have the right of way until they have cleared the crosswalk; drivers must be patient and remain stopped until this happens.

School Zones and Pedestrian Hotspots

Areas around schools, parks, and other recreational spaces are pedestrian hotspots. These zones demand extra caution and a reduced speed, as they are likely to be frequented by children and families. Expect the unexpected and be prepared to yield to pedestrians, particularly children who might not sense the danger and cross unexpectedly.

Shared Spaces and Unmarked Crossing

It's important to recognize that pedestrians' right of way isn't confined solely to marked crosswalks; it applies to all shared spaces, parking lots, or areas without marked crossings. The responsibility of drivers having to yield remains intact. Anticipate pedestrians' movements and give them the space to navigate safely.

Use of Turn Signals—A Precursor to Safe Maneuvers

Communication is critical to seamless movement in the intricate dance of traffic. This chapter unveils an essential aspect of responsible driving—using turn signals well in advance to prevent mishaps and ensure a harmonious flow on California's roads.

Signaling Intentions

Turn signals—those seemingly simple blinking lights on your vehicle —carry a weighty responsibility. They serve as your voice on the road, conveying your intentions to fellow drivers; it can signify a lane change, a turn, or even a merge. By utilizing turn signals effectively, you're ensuring that drivers around you are aware of your plans well before executing them.

The Importance of Timing

The key to appropriately using turn signals lies in the timing of when they are used; for instance, merely activating your turn signal a split second before turning does little to inform other drivers of your intentions. Instead, develop a habit of turning on your turn signal well in advance. The California Vehicle Code requires a minimum of 100 feet before your intended maneuver (DMV, n.d.); this allows other drivers to adjust their speeds and positions, preventing abrupt reactions and potential collisions.

Lane Changes Made Clear

Changing lanes is a prime example of when using your turn signal is critical. It's not just about signaling your intention; it's about ensuring the space you're moving into is available and safe. Before completing a lane change:

- Activate your turn signal.
- Check your side mirror and look over your shoulder to confirm that there is no danger in your blind spot.
- Confidently complete your lane change.

This sequence of actions optimizes safety for you and your fellow drivers.

Merging With Finesse

Turn signals must be used when merging onto freeways. This proactive approach allows drivers in adjacent lanes to make room for you or maintain their speed, allowing for safe merging onto the freeways.

Turn Signal ≠ Right-Of-Way

While turn signals signify intent, it's important to note that they don't grant you an automatic right-of-way; you must still verify if it is safe to proceed with your maneuver and follow the established right-of-way rules.

Preventing Confusion and Mishaps

The core purpose of using turn signals well in advance is to prevent confusion and mishaps. By clearly communicating your intentions, you minimize the risk of misunderstandings that can lead to sudden braking, swerving, or collisions, not only safeguarding you and your passengers but contributing to the overall safety of the road.

EXPLORING THE IMPORTANCE OF RESPECTING OTHER DRIVERS ON THE ROAD

Distracted Driving—Navigating the Perils of Inattention

The Lure of Distraction

The allure of a ringing phone or a blinking screen can be difficult to ignore. But while behind the wheel, a momentary distraction can have grave repercussions. Whether reading a text, typing a reply, or simply checking an app, even a few seconds of distraction from the road can lead to disastrous outcomes.

The Cognitive Burden

Distracted driving is more than simply taking your eyes off the road; it also involves a cognitive load that diverts your attention from the task at hand: safe driving. Texting while behind the wheel is especially dangerous; it demands mental focus that should be dedicated entirely to being a safe driver, minding your surroundings, assessing road conditions, anticipating hazards, and making split-second decisions. The cognitive shift between driving and interacting with a device significantly impairs your ability to react safely and appropriately to unanticipated situations.

Visual and Manual Diversion

Cell phones demand both visual and manual attention. Taking your eyes off the road to glance at a screen or your hands off the wheel to operate a device may only take a fraction of a second. Still, in that time, your vehicle can travel a considerable distance—enough to turn a minor distraction into a major collision. This temporary mental disconnect, often referred to as "tunnel vision," can lead to delayed steering, braking, or accelerating, making it challenging to avoid potential hazards.

The Human Toll

The ramifications of distracted driving extend well beyond the immediate impact. Collisions caused by distracted driving can lead to injuries, fatalities, and irreversible emotional trauma for all parties involved. Lives can be forever altered due to a momentary lapse in attention. As responsible drivers, we must prioritize safety and minimize the risk of harm to ourselves and others.

A Mindful Commitment

It's essential to make a conscious commitment to remain focused to combat the dangers associated with being distracted while behind the wheel. Turn off notifications, stow your phone in a secure spot, and resist the urge to engage with it while driving. If a call or message is urgent, find a safe place to pull over before responding. Remember, the few seconds it takes to respond can wait—unfortunately, your safety and the safety of others cannot.

By fully comprehending the risks and their potential consequences, you're better equipped to make informed decisions. As you traverse California's roads, remember that every moment of attentive driving counts—it's an investment in your safety, the safety of your passengers, and the well-being of fellow road users.

Road Rage—Navigating Stressful Situations With Composure

Being on the road can be challenging: Tempers can flare, and stress can mount. In this chapter, we delve into a critical topic that affects every driver at some point: road rage. As responsible drivers on California's thoroughfares, mastering the art of keeping cool under pressure and avoiding confrontations is paramount for safe and harmonious driving.

Understanding the Trigger

Road rage often stems from a culmination of stressors—traffic congestion, time constraints, personal frustrations—that can lead to an eruption of anger. While these feelings are natural, allowing them to dictate your behavior on the road can escalate situations and endanger everyone involved.

The Ripple Effect

Reacting to road rage with more road rage creates a vicious cycle, contributing to a hostile driving environment. An aggressive gesture, a shouted insult, or an intentional tailgating maneuver can quickly escalate into a dangerous situation. It's crucial to recognize that your actions have a ripple effect on the road culture, affecting not only your safety but the safety of others.

Keeping Cool

Maintaining your composure in the face of road rage requires a conscious effort. Take deep breaths, remind yourself of your ultimate destination, and focus on the bigger picture. When you feel anger rising, acknowledge the emotion without allowing it to control your actions. By cultivating a calm and collected mindset, you position yourself as a responsible and mature driver who prioritizes safety over momentary frustrations.

Avoiding Confrontations

Steering clear of confrontations should be a guiding principle in your driving philosophy. If you encounter an aggressive driver, refrain from responding with aggressive behavior. Avoid eye contact, distance yourself from the situation, and let the aggressor continue on their path. Remember, a sign of strength is to disengage.

De-escalation Techniques

If you find yourself facing an irate driver, consider employing de-escalation techniques. Offering a wave or nod of acknowledgment, rather than an aggressive gesture, can defuse tension. Similarly, allowing an impatient driver to merge in front of you can dissolve their frustration, making it a more positive driving atmosphere.

Report, Don't Retaliate

If you encounter an aggressive driver whose behavior poses a genuine threat, prioritize your safety and the safety of others. Avoid engaging with them and focus on creating distance. If necessary, note their license plate number and report the incident to the authorities. Retaliation only exacerbates the situation and puts everyone on the road at risk.

By remaining composed and level-headed, you wield the power to diffuse tension and create a safer driving environment. The ability to maintain your cool is not a sign of submission; it's a sign of maturity, respect, and a commitment to shared safety. Remember that road rage is a challenge that must be met with patience and restraint. By mastering the art of staying calm under pressure and avoiding confrontations, you're not just protecting yourself, you're contributing to a collective effort that transforms the road from a battlefield of emotions into a space where courtesy, empathy, and safety prevail.

HOW TO APPLY COMMON SENSE WHILE DRIVING

Following the Speed Limit—A Journey in Safe Pace

Designed for Safety

Speed limits are not set arbitrarily; they are established after carefully considering various factors, including road design, traffic flow, and pedestrian activity. Roads are engineered to accommodate specific speeds, taking into account curves, intersections, and potential hazards. Adhering to these limits contributes to a safer road experience for yourself and others.

A Buffer for Reaction Time

Set speed limits account for the time it takes to perceive a hazard, make a decision, and react appropriately. In addition to following another vehicle closer than three seconds, exceeding the speed limit also leaves you with less time to respond to unexpected events. Whether it's a sudden lane change, sudden braking of a vehicle, or an obstacle on the road, driving within the speed limit enhances your ability to react effectively and avoid collisions.

Enhancing Predictability

Consistency in speed helps create a predictable traffic flow. When drivers adhere to speed limits, it minimizes the need for abrupt lane changes, sudden braking, and last-minute decisions. This predictability fosters smoother traffic movement and reduces the likelihood of tailgating, frustration, and road rage.

The Myth of Empty Roads

Even on seemingly empty roads, maintaining the speed limit is imperative. Unforeseen situations can arise at any moment—a pedestrian crossing, an animal darting across the road, or a vehicle suddenly emerging from a side street. Driving above-posted speed limits reduces your ability to respond to these situations promptly and effectively.

Fuel Efficiency and Emissions

Adhering to speed limits enhances safety and contributes to fuel efficiency and reduced emissions. Excessive speed not only wastes fuel but also increases your carbon footprint. By driving at a controlled pace, you're making an environmentally conscious choice.

Setting a Positive Example

As a driver, your actions serve as a model for others on the road. By adhering to speed limits, you encourage a culture of responsible driving that prioritizes safety over impatience. Your commitment to following the rules serves as a testament to your dedication to a safer road environment.

Following the speed limit isn't just a legal obligation; it's a choice that reflects your commitment to responsible and considerate driving.

Driving According to Weather Conditions—Adapting for Safety

Rain and Reduced Traction

When rain graces the roads, it's not just water; it becomes a factor that diminishes traction between your tires and the surface of the road. This reduced grip can lead to longer braking distances and increased chances of skidding. Be aware of the first rains after a dry spell, as all the lubricants and impurities on the road will float to the top and make it more slippery than usual. To navigate rainy conditions safely, reduce your speed, increase following distances, and brake gently. Utilize your headlights for better visibility and avoid sudden maneuvers.

Fog and Limited Visibility

Fog can transform familiar roads into treacherous terrains of limited visibility. In such conditions, slow down and use your low-beam headlights or fog lights to increase your visibility to others. Maintain a safe distance from the vehicle ahead and refrain from using high beams, as they can actually worsen visibility by reflecting off the fog.

Snow and Ice

When driving in areas of snow and ice, the golden rule is to decrease your speed. Snow and ice drastically reduce your tires' traction, making it easier to lose control. Accelerate, brake, and turn gently to avoid skids. Increase your following distance to allow yourself sufficient time to react. If your vehicle starts skidding, steer gently in the direction you want to go, and don't jerk the steering wheel.

Strong Winds and Crosswinds

Wind can be a formidable force on the road, especially on highways and open spaces. When driving in areas of strong winds or crosswinds, maintain a firm grip on the steering wheel and anticipate sudden gusts that can push your vehicle off course. Reduce your speed and exercise caution when passing large vehicles since they may generate wind turbulence.

Hot Weather and Tire Health

High temperatures can impact your tires'

health, leading to blowouts. Inspect the pressure on your tires regularly since heat can lead to increased tire pressure. Avoid overinflating your vehicle's tires, as this can further stress your tires. If you experience a blowout, keep a steady grip on the wheel, gradually decelerate, and pull over to a safe location.

Adapting to Unpredictable Conditions

Weather conditions can change unexpectedly, especially in California's varied climate zones. Check the weather forecast up to and right before starting any trip. If conditions worsen during your drive, consider pulling over at a safe location, such as a rest area, until conditions improve.

Driving in accordance with weather conditions is not merely a recommendation; it's necessary for safety. Your ability to adapt your driving habits to the prevailing weather is a hallmark of responsible and skilled driving. By embracing this flexibility, you're prioritizing safety, minimizing risks, and actively contributing to the overall harmony of California's roads.

From the importance of yielding to pedestrians to the art of using turn signals and staying calm under pressure, these lessons form the bedrock of safe and harmonious road navigation.

Now, armed with a comprehensive understanding of courteous and attentive driving, let's transition into the next phase of our exploration—the realm of road signs. These unspoken guides are vital in keeping us on the right path, ensuring our safety, and facilitating smooth traffic flow. As we delve into the world of road signs, you'll discover how these symbols communicate crucial information, from speed limits to potential hazards.

Embrace the insights you've gained in this chapter and put them into action every time you hit the road.

QUESTIONNAIRE

Let's put your newfound knowledge of common sense rules to the test with some scenario-based questions. Consider each situation carefully and choose the option that aligns best with responsible and considerate driving.

Remember, the choices you make while driving impact your safety and the safety of others. Take your time to consider each scenario and select the option that aligns with responsible and courteous driving practices. Your commitment to applying common sense rules on the road contributes to a safer and more harmonious driving experience for everyone.

Scenario 1: Pedestrian Priority

You're approaching a marked crosswalk where a pedestrian is waiting to cross. What's the appropriate action?

a) Slow down and come to a complete stop to allow the pedestrian to cross.
b) Speed up to cross the crosswalk before the pedestrian starts crossing.
c) Maintain the same speed if the pedestrian makes eye contact.

Scenario 2: Using Turn Signals

You find yourself in heavy traffic and need to change lanes. What should you do?

a) Activate the turn signal and initiate the lane change immediately; the other drivers must yield the right of way to you.
b) Activate your turn signal, sound your horn at least twice, and swiftly switch lanes.
c) Activate your turn signal well in advance, check your mirrors, look over your shoulder, and complete the lane change when it's safe.

Scenario 3: Road Rage

Another driver is tailgating you and honking aggressively. It's best to:

a) Use your brakes abruptly to teach them a lesson.
b) Stay calm, maintain your speed, and let them pass when it's safe.
c) Gesture or shout back at them.

Scenario 4: Following the Speed Limit

You're driving on an empty road where you don't see any other vehicles around. What should you do?

a) Go as fast as you feel it's safe; empty roads are not subject to specific speed limits per the California Vehicle Code.
b) Maintain a speed slightly above the limit, as there's no traffic.
c) Adhere to the posted speed limit, regardless of the absence of other vehicles.

Scenario 5: Adapting to Weather Conditions

Heavy rain has started after a lengthy dry spell, reducing visibility and creating slippery roads. How would you adjust the way you drive?

a) Maintain your typical speed; the first 30 minutes after a dry spell are the safest when it rains.
b) Speed up to get to your destination faster.
c) Slow down and exercise additional caution; the first 30 minutes of rain after a dry spell can be especially slippery. Increase the following distance and use headlights to enhance visibility.

Scenario 6: Distracted Driving

You receive a text message while driving. What's the best course of action?

a) Pull over to the side of the road to respond safely.
b) Read and reply to the message while keeping an eye on the road.
c) Respond to the message quickly while waiting at a red light.

Scenario 7: Right Lane Discipline

You're driving on a multilane road. What's the primary purpose of the right lane?

a) It's meant for high-speed driving and overtaking slower vehicles.

b) It's designated for parked vehicles and is not meant for driving.

c) It's a lane to cruise at a moderate pace, allowing smoother traffic flow.

Scenario 8: Courtesy to Pedestrians

You're approaching an intersection to turn right; a pedestrian is ready to cross the crosswalk. What should you do?

a) Speed through the turn, the pedestrian has lost the right of way by not being proactive and started crossing.

b) Stop completely before the crosswalk, ensuring the pedestrian can cross safely.

c) Slow down slightly but continue the turn without stopping for pedestrians to avoid being rear-ended.

Scenario 9: Merging Onto Highways

You're merging onto a busy highway. How should you enter the traffic flow?

a) Activate your turn signal, adjust your speed to that of the traffic flow, and merge safely into a gap.

b) Bring the vehicle to a complete and sudden stop.

c) Speed up and force your way into a gap; if necessary, lower your window and give a hand gesture to let the other driver know you are going in.

Scenario 10: Dealing With Emergency Vehicles

You're driving on a road, and you hear the sirens of an approaching emergency vehicle (e.g., ambulance, firetruck, police car) behind you. What's the appropriate action?

a) Continue driving at your current speed and let the emergency vehicle find a way around you.

b) Move to the right side of the road and stop.

c) Increase your speed to clear the way for the emergency vehicle as quickly as possible.

Answers

1-a 2-c 3-b 4-c 5-c 6-a 7-c 8-b 9-a 10-b

4

UNDERSTANDING ROAD SIGNS

R oad signs are silent communicators of the roadways, conveying essential information, warnings, and instructions to drivers. As you progress through this chapter, you'll gain a profound understanding of the various types of road signs, from regulatory and warning signs to guide and informational signs. Our approach is both practical and objective, aimed at preparing you to identify these signs effortlessly and respond appropriately in real-life driving scenarios.

Understanding road signs is vital to your overall safety as a driver since road signs serve as a universal language for drivers, bridging the gap between diverse backgrounds and languages. Understanding and adhering to road signs is not just a prerequisite for obtaining your driver's license; it's a fundamental skill that ensures the safety of yourself, your passengers, and other fellow drivers.

At the end of this chapter, you will know how to

- **Identify road signs:** You will become well-versed in recognizing the distinct shapes, colors, symbols, and messages associated with each type of road sign. This ability is crucial for quick and accurate decision-making while driving.
- **Decode their meanings:** We'll delve deep into the meanings behind different categories of road signs, from stop signs that command you to come to a complete stop to speed limit signs that dictate safe driving speeds and caution signs that alert you to potential hazards.
- **Execute appropriate actions:** It's not just about identifying traffic signs; it's about knowing what action to take for each of them. You'll gain the knowledge necessary to be confident to react appropriately to each road sign, whether it's yielding the right-of-way, slowing down, or preparing for a turn.
- **Prepare for real-life driving:** Our objective is to ensure your success on the DMV test and equip you for safe and competent driving in real-life situations. These road signs are not just theoretical concepts; they are tools designed to facilitate safe and responsible driving.

Remember, this chapter is not only about memorization. It's about understanding the rationale behind road signs and integrating that understanding into your driving behavior.

COMPREHENSIVE GUIDE TO ROAD SIGNS

Road signs are the essential language of the road, providing crucial information to drivers. For easy recognition and understanding, let's break down these signs by shape, color, and symbols.

Regulatory Signs

When you encounter them, you must adhere to their instructions without exception. These signs often indicate restrictions or actions you must take.

Shape: Regulatory signs are typically rectangular or circular with varying widths. The longer direction is horizontal.

Color: These signs are white with black or red letters and symbols.

Symbols: Examples include

- **Do not enter sign:** A white horizontal bar within a red circle. This sign signifies that you are prohibited from entering the road or lane.

Warning Signs

These signs demand increased attention and precaution. Adjust your driving accordingly to navigate these hazards safely.

Shape: Warning signs usually have a diamond shape.

Color: These signs are yellow with black symbols and borders.

Symbols: Examples include

- **Curve ahead sign:** Depicts a curving arrow indicating an upcoming curve in the road.
- **Deer crossing sign:** Features an image of a leaping deer, which warns of potential animal crossings.
- **Slippery when wet sign:** Depicts a car skidding on wavy lines. This sign alerts drivers to potentially slippery road conditions when wet.

Guide and Informational Signs

These signs serve as your road companions, assisting you in making informed decisions.

Shape: These signs vary in shape, often rectangular or square.

Color: Guide and informational signs are typically green, blue, or brown with white letters and symbols.

Symbols: Examples include

- **Hospital sign:** Depicts a white "H" on a blue background, indicating nearby medical facilities.
- **Service signs:** Display white symbols on blue backgrounds, indicating services such as rest areas, gas stations, or food.
- **Recreational area sign:** White symbols on brown backgrounds that indicate nearby recreational facilities.

UNDERSTANDING ACTIONS

It's important to remember that road signs are instructions that contribute to the safety and orderliness of our roads. Let's break down the actions each road sign demands, ensuring you're well-prepared for the diverse scenarios you'll encounter.

STOP Sign

When you encounter a STOP sign, it's non-negotiable. You must come to a complete stop before crossing the limit line; when no limit line is present, then stop before entering the intersection. Ensure the way is clear, and only proceed when it's safe to do so. For maximum safety, please be alert that many drivers treat stop  signs as yield signs and do "slow rolls" or a mere tap on the brakes and continue without coming to a complete stop.

YIELD Sign

 A YIELD sign mandates giving the right-of-way to other vehicles or pedestrians. While you don't have to come to a complete stop, you must slow down, be prepared to stop if necessary, and give way to those with the right of way.

"NO" Signs

These signs, usually circular with a red border and a black symbol or text, indicate prohibited actions. When you see a "NO" road sign, the action depicted within the road sign is not permitted.

No U-Turn Sign

When you come across a "NO U-Turn" sign, it's clear: making a U-turn at that point is prohibited. Not respecting this sign can result in a collision with another driver or harm a pedestrian; keep driving and perform the U-turn at a place where it's legal to do so.

No Left Turn Sign

A "NO Left Turn" sign is clear. It means you are not allowed to make a left turn at the indicated location. Plan your route accordingly to avoid left turns where this sign is present.

No Right Turn Sign

Similar to the "NO Left Turn" sign, the "NO Right Turn" sign prohibits making a right turn at the specified location. Abide by this sign's instruction and find an appropriate place to turn right.

No Right Turn on Red Sign

Right turns are permitted only when the light is green. You must wait for the light to turn green before making a right turn, regardless of whether you consider it safe.

School Signs

School signs advise drivers of the presence of a school zone. These signs indicate reduced speed limits when children are likely to be present. Be prepared to slow down and exercise heightened caution in these areas.

Railroad Crossing Signs

When you encounter a railroad crossing sign, it signifies an upcoming railroad crossing. Slow down, prepare to stop if necessary, and ensure the tracks are clear before proceeding. Note that uncontrolled railroad signs have a 15-mile-per-hour speed limit.

CHANGES IN ROAD SIGNS

Drivers must remain up-to-date on road sign changes. Not doing so jeopardizes their overall safety; local news media and the California Department of Motor Vehicles website are good sources of information to stay current on road sign changes.

Evolving Road Conditions

Roads are constantly evolving, from construction and expansion projects to changes in traffic flow patterns. As a result, the need for effective communication with drivers becomes paramount. New or temporary road signs are typically used in these scenarios to ensure that drivers remain safe.

Advances in Traffic Management

Traffic management techniques and technologies are in a constant state of evolution; therefore, new road signs might be introduced to improve overall road safety and optimize traffic flow.

Addressing Safety Concerns

The primary purpose of road signs is safety. Suppose authorities identify areas with higher accident rates or specific safety concerns. In that case, they might introduce new road signs or modify existing ones to mitigate risks and prevent accidents.

Legal and Regulatory Changes

Traffic laws and regulations are subject to change over time. Therefore, new road signs are typically used to keep drivers informed about these changes, assuring drivers are up-to-date with their rights and responsibilities.

Urban Planning and Development

Urban planning and development can lead to changes in traffic patterns. New signs may be introduced to guide drivers through newly developed areas, directing them to essential services and ensuring smooth navigation.

THE ADVANTAGES OF TRAFFIC SIGNS

Clear Communication

Road signs provide a standardized and clear way to communicate essential information to drivers. Whether it's indicating speed limits, guiding through complex intersections, or warning about hazards, signs ensure that drivers receive crucial information at a glance.

Universal Language

Road signs transcend language barriers. They provide a universal language that all drivers can understand, regardless of their native language, ensuring consistent communication across diverse communities.

Enhancing Predictability

Consistent road signs enhance predictability for drivers. When drivers know what to expect, they can make informed decisions, reducing the likelihood of abrupt maneuvers or collisions and increasing overall road safety.

Supporting Decision-Making

Traffic signs assist drivers in making quick decisions on the road. They provide timely information about speed limits, directions, potential hazards, and more, empowering drivers to navigate complex situations confidently.

Promoting Order and Safety

By guiding drivers and setting expectations, road signs contribute to orderly traffic flow and reduce the risk of accidents. They create a standardized environment that promotes safe and responsible driving behavior.

As drivers, it's essential to recognize that road signs are not static elements. They evolve to meet each roadway's changing demands and enhance overall safety. Staying updated on these changes through resources like the California DMV handbook, official websites, and driving education programs is crucial. By embracing these changes, you demonstrate a commitment to being a responsible and adaptable driver, contributing to the overall well-being of everyone on the road.

Understanding why road signs are essential goes beyond the DMV test—it's about fostering responsible and conscientious driving habits that contribute to the well-being of all road users.

At the core, road signs are a tool for safety. They provide crucial information that helps drivers anticipate and respond to potential hazards. Whether it's a warning about a sharp curve ahead or indicating a school zone, these signs play a pivotal role in accident prevention and protecting lives. They serve as a method for ensuring orderly traffic flow. They inform drivers about speed limits, right-of-way rules, and directional guidance, reducing the likelihood of confusion and conflicts on the road.

In a diverse and multicultural society like California, road signs provide a standardized way of communicating information to all drivers, regardless of their background or language proficiency, like navigational guides assisting drivers in reaching their destinations safely and efficiently. They indicate things upcoming like turns, exits, and landmarks or rest areas, to name a few, making navigation simpler for both local and unfamiliar drivers.

Drivers adhering to road signs contribute to a predictable driving environment. This predictability reduces the likelihood of sudden maneuvers, ultimately lowering the risk of accidents. Comprehending them is a fundamental aspect of driver education. Learning to interpret and respond to signs prepares new drivers for real-world road scenarios, building their confidence and competence.

NEWS AND MEDIA

Staying updated with the latest changes and developments related to road signs is crucial for drivers. While the basics of road signs remain consistent, changes and updates can occur for various reasons, including safety improvements, legal amendments, and advancements in traffic management.

New regulations or modifications to existing laws can lead to changes in road signs. Keeping up with news and official sources helps you stay aware of these changes and understand how they might impact your driving behavior.

Incorporating the habit of staying updated through credible news sources and official channels enhances your driving proficiency.

From the commanding STOP sign to the informative guide signs that lead us to hospitals, services, and recreational areas, we've deciphered the language of various road signs. We've explored the shapes, colors, symbols, and messages that form the foundation of road communication.

Beyond mere identification, we've grasped the significance of adhering to the actions each sign dictates. We have recognized that road signs are not static; they adapt to changing road conditions, advances in traffic management, and evolving safety concerns. Now that you're equipped with an understanding of road signs, it's time to translate this knowledge into real-world action. As you take the wheel, remember that every road sign carries a purpose, a message aimed at your safety and the safety of others. Be vigilant, observe, and respond to road signs attentively and confidently.

With this chapter as your guide, you've equipped yourself with a foundation beyond passing your DMV test. By consistently adhering to road signs, you'll contribute to the orderliness and harmony of our roads, creating a safer driving environment for everyone.

As we move on to the next chapter, "Best Driving Practices," consider this a continuation of your journey toward becoming a proficient and responsible driver. So, get ready to explore the principles that will guide you through the intricacies of real-life driving scenarios.

QUESTIONNAIRE

To solidify your understanding of road signs, let's put your knowledge to the test with some practice questions. Get ready to challenge yourself and enhance your road sign recognition skills.

1. A "STOP" sign requires you to:

    a) Stop completely.
    b) Slow down and proceed with caution.
    c) Yield the right-of-way to other vehicles.
    d) Turn left at the intersection.

2. What does a "YIELD" sign mean?

a) The right-of-way is yours.
b) Come to a stop.
c) Reduce speed and, if needed, stop to give the right of way.
d) Proceed without any restrictions.

3. What does a round "NO U-Turn" sign signify?

a) You can make a U-turn ahead.
b) A U-turn is not allowed.
c) U-turns are allowed only during specific hours.
d) U-turns are permitted, provided there is no oncoming traffic within 200 feet.

4. A sign that is blue with a white "H" signifies?

a) Nearby gas station.
b) Upcoming school zone.
c) Rest area ahead.
d) Nearby medical facility or hospital.

5. Signs that are yellow diamond-shaped typically indicate?

a) Speed limits for the area.
b) Upcoming hazards or warnings.
c) Directional guidance to nearby cities.
d) Locations of recreational areas.

Keep up the great work! In the next chapter, we'll delve into "Best Driving Practices," building on the foundation you've established here and helping you navigate real-life driving situations with confidence and competence.

Answers
1. a) 2. c) 3. b) 4. d) 5. b)

5

BEST DRIVING PRACTICES

It is amazing how many drivers, even at the Formula One level, think that the brakes are for slowing the car down.

— MARIO ANDRETTI

Just like Andretti said, by using the brakes to slow the car down, it allows the driver better control of the vehicle. Throughout this guidebook, you've undoubtedly acquired a solid foundation of knowledge about the rules and regulations that govern our roads. Now, it's time to delve into the heart of responsible and safe driving—the realm of best driving practices.

It's time for you to explore the art of driving beyond the rules—a skill that involves understanding the nuances of the road, appreciating the diverse conditions it presents, and adapting your driving, ensuring your safety and the safety of other drivers and pedestrians. The true essence of driving goes beyond mechanical skills; it encompasses a mindful approach that considers the ever-changing dynamics of the road and weather.

Driving is an activity that demands not just knowing how to operate a vehicle—it requires a profound comprehension to treat the road as a living entity. It needs to be treated as such because roads are constantly in flux. Traffic patterns shift, pedestrians emerge, weather conditions change, and unexpected situations unfold. The synergy between your skill as a driver and your ability to adapt will define your success on the road.

In this chapter, we will journey through the realms of the best driving practices with an objective and realistic perspective. Our goal is to equip you with the knowledge that is pivotal to your safety and the safety of others. While the DMV exam may evaluate your understanding of rules, this chapter extends beyond that examination. Here, we delve into the uncharted territories of practical wisdom—the knowledge you will attain through experience and a willingness to learn.

Our goal is to foster within you a genuine appreciation for the significance of adopting good driving habits. Together, we will uncover the critical elements of safe driving that will make you a responsible driver and instill the confidence to navigate through various scenarios, be it congested city streets, winding mountain roads, or rain-soaked highways.

So, open your mind to the dynamic nature of the road, the ever-changing conditions it throws your way, and the proactive measures you can apply, ensuring the safety and well-being of all those who share it with you. Let's embark on this enlightening journey to master the best driving practices that will serve you well on California's roads and beyond.

GOOD DRIVING HABITS

It's crucial to understand that the nuances of the road extend far beyond the lines on the pavement. It's the small, consistent habits that truly make a difference in ensuring not only your safety but also the safety of those around you.

Maintaining a Safe Following Distance

Vehicles need room to maneuver safely. One of the most fundamental habits to adopt is maintaining a safe following distance—a buffer zone between you and the vehicle ahead of you. This space provides you with precious moments to react should the unexpected occur.

The "three-second rule" is the safety buffer recommended for a following distance. A way to test if you are adhering to the "three-second rule" is to choose a stationary object along the roadside; when the vehicle ahead of you is passing that object, start counting: "one-thousand-one, one-thousand-two, one-thousand-three." If your vehicle passes the same object before you finish counting, you're following too closely. Increase your following distance to allow for adequate response time. This distance should be increased based on road conditions and weather (DMV, 2019).

Checking Blind Spots: The Hidden Dangers

Blind spots are the areas outside your immediate field of vision where other vehicles or motorcyclists may lurk undetected. Cultivating the practice of checking your blind spots before changing lanes or making a turn is a vital skill.

Before maneuvering, carefully look over your shoulder to ensure there's no vehicle hiding in your blind spot. Utilize your mirrors but remember they don't capture everything. A simple, deliberate check can prevent a collision and keep surprises at bay.

USING TURN SIGNALS CORRECTLY: COMMUNICATING INTENT

Turn signals are your voice on the road, conveying your intentions to fellow drivers. Using them correctly enhances predictability and reduces confusion. No matter if you're changing lanes, merging onto a highway, or making a turn, remember to signal your intentions well in advance.

Signal at least 100 feet before a turn in city driving and 300 feet on the highway (DMV, n.d.). Ensure your signal is off after the maneuver to avoid misleading other drivers. Remember, using your turn signals isn't just a rule—it's a courteous act that contributes to the flow and safety of traffic.

SAFETY GUIDELINES FOR DRIVING ON CALIFORNIA'S BUSY HIGHWAYS: DRIVING WITH CONFIDENCE

Driving in the bustling landscape of California's highways requires a unique blend of skill, alertness, and adaptability.

Maintain a Smooth and Consistent Speed

On California's highways, traffic often ebbs and flows like the tides. To ensure a safe and harmonious journey, strive to maintain a smooth and consistent speed. Abrupt changes in velocity can lead to unnecessary braking, causing a chain reaction of slowdowns.

Use Your Mirrors Vigilantly

Your mirrors are your allies on the highway—they grant you a broader perspective of your surroundings. Make it a habit to check your mirrors regularly, especially before changing lanes, merging, or making sudden maneuvers. This practice not only keeps you informed about approaching vehicles but also instills confidence in your decision-making.

Adjust your mirrors to minimize blind spots but remember that they don't capture everything. A quick glance over your shoulder, as mentioned in earlier sections, is a prudent double-check before changing lanes.

Anticipate Traffic Flow

California highways can transform from free-flowing to congested in the blink of an eye. Developing the ability to anticipate traffic flow is a skill that comes with experience. Observe the behavior of vehicles ahead—if you notice a gradual slowing, ease off the accelerator early to allow for a smooth deceleration. This proactive approach reduces the need for sudden braking and contributes to a safer driving environment for everyone.

Merge With Caution

Merging onto a busy highway is a dance of cooperation. Timing and communication are key. Use your turn signals well in advance, match your speed with the flow of traffic, and identify a suitable gap to merge into. Strive to enter the highway without disrupting the flow and remember that existing traffic has the right-of-way.

Prepare for Weather Variability

California's diverse climate demands adaptability. From the glaring sun to sudden rain showers, be prepared for the spectrum of weather conditions. Adjust your driving style to accommodate reduced visibility, slippery roads, and longer stopping distances during inclement weather.

In mastering these good driving habits, you're not only refining your skills but also nurturing a sense of responsibility that extends to every mile you cover. The road is a shared space, and it's through these small yet significant habits that we build a community of conscientious drivers. As you internalize these practices, you'll find yourself not just passing a test but truly embodying the essence of safe, courteous, and confident driving.

ADAPTING TO WEATHER

In California, weather plays a significant role; various weather conditions require adaptability and vigilance. Let's explore the art of adapting to different weather conditions. This skill ensures your safety and preserves the well-being of everyone sharing the road.

Fog: Peering Through the Mist

Fog can obscure your surroundings, transforming familiar roads into a challenging maze. When encountering foggy conditions, it's crucial to adjust your driving behavior to ensure a safe journey by doing the following:

- **Reduce speed:** Gradually slowdown in accordance with your visibility. Fog impairs distance perception, and driving slower, allowing you to see better through the fog, gives you more time to react to sudden obstacles.
- **Use low-beam headlights:** Switch on your low-beam headlights to improve your visibility while minimizing glare. High beams typically reflect off the fog, causing reduced visibility.
- **Increase following distance:** Give yourself more than the three-second following distance to see stopped vehicles or hazards more quickly as they emerge through the fog. The fog may mask brake lights, requiring extra time for a safe stop.
- **Stay cautious at intersections:** Approach intersections with extreme caution. Cross-traffic might be challenging to see; therefore, reduce speed and be prepared to yield or stop if necessary.

Rain: Navigating Slippery Slopes

Rain can transform roadways into slick surfaces, testing your ability to maintain control and awareness. To navigate rainy conditions safely, consider these strategies:

- **Turn on headlights:** Rain decreases visibility, so turn on your headlights to enhance your visibility and make your vehicle more conspicuous to others.
- **Increase following distance:** Rain creates longer stopping distances. Increase the distance between you and the vehicle ahead to ensure you have adequate braking time.
- **Smooth and gentle maneuvers:** Sudden maneuvers can lead to skidding. Brake, accelerate, and steer gently to maintain control. Think of how you walk when the sidewalk is wet; you are more careful not to make any sudden maneuvers that may cause you to slip and fall, correct? Apply the same common sense for driving in the rain.
- **Watch for hydroplaning:** When water accumulates on the road's surface, your tires can lose contact with the pavement, leading to hydroplaning. If this happens, ease off the accelerator and steer straight until you regain control. Do not use your brakes while hydroplaning, as this may cause total loss of control.

Snow: Treading the Icy Path

Snow-covered roads present an intricate challenge, requiring a delicate balance between control and caution. When driving in snowy conditions, remember:

- **Use winter tires:** Put on winter tires or chains for improved traction if possible. Regular tires usually don't provide sufficient traction on icy surfaces.

- **Reduce speed further:** Snowy roads demand even slower speeds. Accelerate, brake, and steer gradually to minimize the risk of skidding.
- **Increase your following distance dramatically:** The stopping distance on snow can be significantly longer. Maintain a substantial gap between you and the vehicle in front.
- **Use lower gears:** When descending steep hills, shift to a lower gear to reduce the risk of skidding due to rapid acceleration.

As you navigate the diverse weather conditions of California, remember that adaptation is the key to a safe journey. Embrace the ever-changing elements as opportunities to refine your driving techniques and uphold the responsibility we all share on the road.

ADAPTING TO ROAD CONDITIONS

Each road holds its own narrative and rhythm, demanding your skill and adaptability to ensure your safety and the well-being of other drivers.

The Importance of Road Conditions While Driving

The road is your driving partner, influencing your every turn, stop, and acceleration. Recognizing and adapting to changing road conditions is a skilled and responsible driver trait.

Navigating Uneven Roads: A Smooth Approach

Uneven roads are a frequent companion on your journey, and they demand a measured approach to maintain control and comfort.

- **Reduce speed:** Slow down when encountering uneven surfaces, allowing your vehicle's suspension to absorb the road unevenness and offer a smoother ride.

- **Maintain a steady grip:** Keep a firm but relaxed grip on the steering wheel. Avoid sudden jerks or tight gripping, as these can amplify the impact of bumps.
- **Adjust following distance:** Maintain a slightly greater following distance when driving on uneven roads, giving you extra time to react if your vehicle responds unexpectedly to the road's contours.

Navigating Potholes: Evading the Pitfalls

Potholes can turn an uneventful drive into a challenge, threatening your vehicle's stability and potentially causing damage.

- **Stay alert:** Keep a watchful eye on the road ahead. Potholes can appear suddenly, and your ability to anticipate them is crucial.
- **Reduce speed:** Slow down when approaching areas with pothole potential. Lowering your speed will give you more time to react and maneuver around them.
- **Maintain tire pressure:** Properly inflated tires are more resilient to impact. Inspect your tire pressure regularly to lessen the risk of damage.

Navigating Road Construction Areas: A Passage of Caution

Construction zones can disrupt the flow of traffic and present hazards that demand heightened vigilance.

WARNING

CONSTRUCTION AREA

- **Follow signage:** Adhere to posted speed limits and any

construction-related signage. Reduced speed limits are often in place to ensure the safety of everyone on the road, including the workers.

- **Merge early:** Follow merge instructions well in advance of lane closures. Sudden lane changes can lead to confusion and potential collisions.
- **Stay calm and patient:** Road work zones can test your patience, but maintaining a composed attitude contributes to a safer environment for everyone.

As you navigate California's varied terrain, remember that your adaptability is a hallmark of responsible driving. The road conditions may change, but your commitment to safety and awareness must remain steadfast.

CITY VS. RURAL DRIVING: NAVIGATING DIVERSE LANDSCAPES

It's essential to recognize that the road's character transforms as you transition from cityscapes to rural expanses. Each setting presents unique challenges that push the driver's skill set to ensure safe navigation.

City Driving: Navigating Urban Labyrinths

Driving in the heart of a bustling city demands a heightened sense of awareness and adaptability.

In city driving, you'll encounter heavy traffic that often tests your patience and planning. Traffic signals, stop signs, and pedestrian crossings necessitate precise timing and awareness. Remember, pedestrians, cyclists, and motorcyclists are abundant in urban areas. Always anticipate unexpected movements from non-motorized road users and exercise caution at crosswalks.

Additionally, frequent lane changes and parallel parking are often required in city driving. To master these maneuvers, use your mirrors and use turn signals appropriately. Practice smooth lane changes to maintain traffic flow while being attentive to other drivers.

Rural Driving: Embracing Open Spaces

Rural roads offer a departure from the urban frenzy, replacing it with open vistas and unique challenges.

When driving in rural areas, be prepared for the potential of limited services. Gas stations and amenities might be fewer and farther between. Plan your fuel stops and refreshment breaks accordingly to ensure you aren't stranded.

Unpredictable wildlife encounters are another aspect of rural driving. Animals can unexpectedly venture onto rural roads, especially during dawn and dusk. Stay vigilant and reduce your speed if you spot wildlife or notice road signs indicating potential animal crossings.

Rural roads tend to be narrower, so exercise patience and use designated turnouts when necessary to allow faster-moving vehicles to pass safely.

A HERO'S JOURNEY THROUGH THE STORM: A LESSON IN PREPAREDNESS

Real-life stories often emerge as powerful lessons, showcasing the importance of knowledge and preparedness. Let's delve into a heartwarming narrative that exemplifies the impact of prior understanding in tackling challenging driving situations, especially in the face of adverse weather conditions, as provided by Cook (2023).

Meet Jon Gilbert, a seasoned driver who had navigated various roadways for years. One winter's day, a sudden and intense snowstorm descended upon the city, blanketing the streets and highways with treacherous ice. As the city grappled with the sudden freeze, Jon found himself on a perilous journey that would put his driving skills to the ultimate test.

Driving along an icy off-ramp, Jon encountered a scene of chaos. More than 20 vehicles were stranded, their tires slipping and sliding, unable to gain traction on the slippery surface. Traffic had come to a standstill, and the situation seemed dire. However, Jon's years of experience and the wisdom he had accumulated from his driving education courses kicked into action.

As he navigated the icy terrain, he noticed something remarkable. Rather than focusing solely on his journey, he felt a surge of compassion for the stranded drivers around him. He realized he had the skills to help, so he decided to take action.

Jon cautiously approached the off-ramp, drawing from his understanding of safe winter driving. He helped many stranded and freezing people by bringing food and helping them free up their cars that had become stuck in the zone.

Jon assessed the situation, donned his winter gear, and began assisting fellow drivers in need. Armed with his knowledge of how to free stuck vehicles from ice, he used techniques he had learned in his driving education class to help drivers rock their cars gently and strategically to regain traction.

One by one, Jon's efforts bore fruit—he helped free vehicle after vehicle from the icy grip of the off-ramp. His patience, experience, and prior understanding proved invaluable as the hours passed. His actions not only facilitated the flow of traffic but also showcased the power of preparedness in the face of adversity.

Jon's journey that day was more than just a drive through a snowstorm; it was a testament to the impact of responsible driving practices. His story underscores the importance of being equipped with the knowledge to navigate even the most challenging conditions. Through his actions, he demonstrated the power of preparedness. He exemplified the spirit of community and responsibility that defines safe and conscientious driving.

Remember, these practices are the tools that enable you to respond adeptly to real-world situations. By internalizing the principles shared in this chapter, you're well-prepared to navigate the complexities of city and rural driving, handle inclement weather, and embrace the dynamics of freeway travel.

As you move forward, put these ideas into action. The true measure of these practices lies in their implementation on the road. Remember the techniques you've learned here the next time you encounter heavy traffic, a dense fog, or a potholed road. Approach each situation with the confidence and preparedness that come from understanding.

Safe driving practices are just half of the picture. In our next chapter, "Driver Responsibility and Consequences," we'll delve into the legal and social responsibilities you shoulder as a driver and the potential consequences of not following the rules of the road. By understanding the importance of responsible driving behavior, you'll continue to build a foundation of knowledge and behavior that elevates your driving to a higher standard.

So, as you navigate the path ahead, carry the insights of this chapter with you. Let your driving be a testament to your commitment to safety, responsibility, and the well-being of all road users. With every mile you cover, you contribute to a culture of responsible driving, making the road a safer place for everyone.

CHOOSE YOUR OWN DRIVING ADVENTURE

Welcome to the *Choose Your Own Driving Adventure* game, where you get to put your newfound knowledge of best driving practices to the test! As you navigate through different driving scenarios, remember the principles you've learned in this chapter. Select the option that you believe is the best driving practice for each situation. Let's begin!

Scenario 1: City Traffic Challenge

While driving through heavy city traffic, the vehicle ahead of you abruptly comes to a stop. What's the best driving practice?

a) Honk and slam on the brakes.
b) Keep an ample following distance and gently use your brakes.
c) Quickly change lanes to avoid the stopped vehicle.

Scenario 2: Foggy Conditions

You're driving through thick fog where visibility is severely reduced. What's the best driving practice?

a) Turn on your high beams to see better.
b) Increase your speed to pass through the fog faster.
c) Reduce your speed, turn on your low beams, and maintain a safe following distance.

Scenario 3: Rural Road Encounter

While driving on a narrow rural road, you see a group of pedestrians walking along the side. What's the best driving practice?

a) Reduce your speed and provide ample space for the pedestrians by moving over to the opposite lane if it's safe to do so.
b) Slow down and honk your horn to alert the pedestrians of your presence.
c) Continue driving at your current speed. Pedestrians should stay on the sidewalk.

Scenario 4: Icy Road Ahead

You approach a stretch of road covered in ice. What's the best driving practice?

a) Continue driving at your current speed. Your vehicle can handle the ice.
b) Accelerate to get through the icy section more quickly.
c) Lower your speed and maintain a safe distance.

Scenario 5: Freeway Driving

You're on a busy freeway, your exit is 2 miles away and you need to make two lane changes for your exit. What's the best driving practice?

a) Force your way into traffic to make your exit, regardless of the other vehicles.
b) Remain calm, use your turn signal, and make the lane changes one at a time when you find a suitable gap.
c) Slow down and stop if necessary until the other drivers stop as well so you can change lanes.

Scenario 6: Pothole Alert

You spot a deep pothole ahead on the road. What's the best driving practice?

a) Swerve sharply to avoid the pothole, even if it means crossing into another lane.
b) Brace for impact and drive straight over the pothole to minimize vehicle damage.
c) Lower your speed, check your mirrors, and cautiously drive around the pothole.

Your choices reflect your understanding of best driving practices and your commitment to safe and responsible driving. Remember, real-life driving situations may not always have clear-cut options, but your knowledge will guide you in making the right decisions. Keep honing your skills and applying the principles you've learned to ensure a safe and enjoyable driving experience for yourself and others on the road.

Answers:
Scenario 1-b Scenario 2-c Scenario 3-aScenario 4-c Scenario 5-b Scenario 6-c

Back to the Labyrinth...

The difficulty in dealing with a maze or labyrinth lies not so much in navigating the convolutions to find the exit but in not entering the damn thing in the first place.

— VERA NAZARIAN

We talked about the DMV as a labyrinth in the introduction for a reason: It's because when you have it ahead of you, a barrier to the freedom of the open road, that's exactly how it seems. But as you're discovering, no labyrinth is impossible to figure out. You just need to put down your panic and figure out the direction step by step.

The real problem with the California DMV Exam is not its contents or its difficulty: It's the fact that it terrifies people before they even set out. A labyrinth *seems* impossible to get through when you're looking at it all at once and it's standing in the way of your goal, but it's not really.

Of course, there are plenty of study guides out there that help you memorize answers, but as you've probably found yourself, that only adds to your stress. This approach, as you know, is different, and this is your chance to help other people get rid of that fear and find their way through the labyrinth calmly and confidently.

By leaving a review of this book on Amazon, you'll show other worried drivers exactly where they can find all the guidance they need to not only be road-ready, but to seize the opportunity ahead.

Your review will help new readers find the comprehensive guidance they're really looking for and show them that the DMV isn't as much of a barrier as they fear.

Thank you for your support. You're providing peace of mind and guidance for other drivers – and you're also contributing to a new wave of responsible and confident drivers on the road.

Scan the QR code to leave a review!

6

DRIVER RESPONSIBILITY AND CONSEQUENCES

A dream doesn't become reality through magic; it takes sweat, determination, and hard work.

— COLIN POWELL

As a responsible driver, your obligations go far beyond simply maneuvering a vehicle from point A to point B. Understanding and embracing your responsibilities as a driver is not only a legal requirement but also a moral duty that contributes to the safety and harmony of our roads.

Driving is a privilege that carries a significant weight of responsibility. Beyond the mechanical operation of a vehicle, you're responsible for your safety and the safety of your passengers and others sharing the road. Understanding the rules of the road and adhering to traffic laws are not just legal obligations but also ethical commitments that demonstrate your respect for the lives and well-being of others.

Throughout this chapter, we will explore the consequences that can arise from violations of traffic rules. These consequences extend beyond mere fines and penalties; they can encompass life-altering events affecting your driving record, insurance rates, and personal freedom. By understanding the potential aftermath of driving rule violations, you will be better equipped to make thoughtful decisions prioritizing safety and compliance.

Insurance serves as a crucial safety net in the realm of driving responsibilities. We will cover the various types of insurance coverage available to drivers and emphasize the importance of maintaining adequate coverage. Understanding how insurance works and its role in mitigating financial burdens for yourself and those you impact resulting from accidents is vital to you being a responsible driver.

Our intention with this chapter is to foster a deep sense of responsibility among drivers. A well-informed driver is empowered and capable of making choices that positively impact their safety and that of others. By recognizing the far-reaching consequences of our driving actions on the road, we can collectively contribute to a safe, courteous, and law-abiding culture.

By the end of this chapter, you will have gained a profound comprehension of the multifaceted responsibilities associated with being a driver. You will be well-informed about the potential repercussions that follow when these responsibilities are disregarded. We aim to provide you with a clear and objective understanding of the legal and ethical obligations that come with the privilege of driving. By knowing these obligations, you will be better equipped to make informed decisions on the road, minimize risks, and contribute to a safer driving environment.

So, let's delve into driver responsibility and consequences as we equip you with the knowledge and insights necessary for a lifetime of responsible and mindful driving.

LEGAL AND MORAL RESPONSIBILITIES

Legal Obligations

Driving a vehicle isn't solely about steering, accelerating, and braking. It entails a set of legal obligations that every driver must abide by to ensure the safety and orderliness of our roads. These obligations are in place not only to protect you but also to safeguard the lives of those sharing the road with you.

- **Adhering to traffic laws:** Part of being a responsible driver is having a comprehensive understanding of the traffic laws governing the state of California; including following speed limits, obeying traffic signs and signals, yielding the right-of-way, and performing full stops at stop signs and red lights. Ignoring these laws not only puts you at risk of legal penalties but also jeopardizes the safety of everyone on the road.
- **Driving sober:** One of the most crucial legal responsibilities is to drive sober. Driving under the influence of alcohol or drugs is unlawful as it poses a significant threat to your safety and that of others on the road. Getting behind the wheel while impaired negatively affects judgment, reflexes, and decision-making abilities, significantly increasing the likelihood of accidents with catastrophic outcomes.
- **Maintaining a valid driver's license:** Obtaining a driver's license is a privilege and a legal requirement to drive a motor vehicle. It signifies that you've met the qualifications and demonstrated your ability to drive safely. It's crucial to renew your license on time and adhere to any restrictions or endorsements specified on it.

Moral Responsibilities

In addition to the legal obligations, a set of moral responsibilities comes with being a driver. These responsibilities reflect the law and your ethical duty to contribute to a harmonious and safe driving environment.

- **Respecting other drivers' safety:** Every driver on the road is entitled to a safe journey. Meaning drivers should not engage in aggressive or reckless behaviors that could endanger their lives; instead, they should follow behaviors that promote safety, such as maintaining a safe following distance, using turn signals appropriately, and refraining from distractions while driving.
- **Making ethical decisions on the road:** The road is full of unexpected situations that require split-second decisions. Ethical decisions involve putting the safety and well-being of others before any personal inconvenience; examples are allowing pedestrians to cross, yielding to emergency vehicles, and choosing to drive cautiously in adverse weather conditions. Remember that the roads are a shared space, and each driver's actions influence that space's overall safety and orderliness.

It's essential to recognize that being a responsible driver entails a commitment to the law and the well-being of others, ultimately leading to a more secure and cooperative driving environment for all.

DRIVING WITHOUT A LICENSE: CALIFORNIA VEHICLE CODE SECTION 12951 VC

Understanding that having a driver's license is a privilege makes it vital to discuss the ramifications of driving without a valid driver's license. California Vehicle Code Section 12951 VC addresses the offense of failing to show a driver's license when operating a motor vehicle. This section underscores the significance of always carrying a valid driver's license while driving.

California Vehicle Code Section 12951 VC says anyone who operates a motor vehicle must have their driver's license in their possession and must present it to a peace officer at their request; this is essential for verifying that drivers are authorized to operate a vehicle and have met the necessary qualifications.

Not being able to present a valid driver's license as required by California Vehicle Code Section 12951 VC can lead to numerous legal consequences. It's imperative to understand that these consequences are in place to encourage responsible and compliant behavior among drivers.

- **Legal penalties:** If you cannot present a valid driver's license upon request by a law enforcement officer, you may face legal penalties. These penalties could include fines, which may vary depending on the circumstances, including any prior violations.
- **Impact on driving record:** Violations in this section can result in points added to your driving record. Accumulating points on your record can lead to higher insurance rates and a potential driver's license suspension if the points exceed a certain threshold within a specified timeframe.
- **Compromised insurance:** Driving without a valid driver's license can impact your insurance coverage. In the event of an accident, car insurance companies may use your lack of a valid driver's license as grounds to deny coverage, leaving you personally responsible for any resulting damages or liabilities.

California Vehicle Code Section 12951 VC states driving without a driver's license is an infraction. Be sure to follow this regulation to avoid legal consequences and contribute to our roads' overall safety and accountability.

Understanding the legal obligations outlined in California Vehicle Code Section 12951 VC is paramount in our commitment to promoting responsible and informed driving. Adhering to these regulations collectively contributes to a safer driving environment for all road users.

ALCOHOL AND DRUGS: ETHICAL DECISION MAKING BEHIND THE WHEEL—A DRIVING SIMULATOR STUDY

Alcohol and drugs are substances that can significantly impair a driver's abilities, leading to compromised judgment, coordination, and reaction times. It's crucial to acknowledge that operating a vehicle while under the influence is not only a legal violation but also an irresponsible action that jeopardizes the safety of oneself and others on the road.

The Driving Simulator Study: Ethical Decision-Making

The driving simulator study discussed in this chapter aimed to explore how drivers make ethical decisions when confronted with situations involving alcohol or drugs. This study placed participants in various simulated scenarios, assessing their choices when presented with opportunities to avoid driving under the influence (Samuel, et. al., 2020).

Study Outcomes: Ethical Dilemmas and Responsible Choices

The driving simulator study yielded important insights into the ethical dilemmas drivers encounter and the decisions they make under the influence of substances. Some outcomes included

- **Impaired judgment:** Participants who consumed alcohol or drugs in the simulated scenarios exhibited poor judgment, leading them to underestimate the risks of driving under the influence.

- **Increased risk-taking:** The study revealed that under the influence, participants were more likely to engage in risky behaviors such as speeding, weaving between lanes, and failing to obey traffic signals.
- **Inhibited reaction times:** Driving simulator data indicated that alcohol and drugs hindered participants' ability to react promptly to unexpected events on the road.
- **Ethical decision-making:** Despite the impairments caused by substances, some participants exhibited responsible, ethical decision-making by opting not to drive and seeking alternative modes of transportation.

IMPLICATIONS FOR RESPONSIBLE DRIVING

The outcomes of the driving simulator study underscore the critical importance of responsible decision-making when it comes to alcohol and drugs. The study reinforces the idea that driving under the influence endangers lives and reflects a lapse in ethical judgment.

As responsible drivers, it's imperative to draw from the study's insights and prioritize safety above all else, refraining from driving if you've consumed alcohol or drugs, and actively seeking alternative options such as designated drivers or rideshare services. By making ethical choices, you contribute to a safer driving environment and uphold the responsibilities of being a licensed driver.

Consequences of Violations: California Traffic Ticket Fines and Penalties

Traffic citation fines serve as a means of discouraging rule violations and promoting responsible driving behavior. Fines vary based on the offense's nature, the violation's severity, and any prior infractions. It's vital to recognize that fines are not merely financial consequences but also to make drivers reconsider their actions and encourage adherence to the law.

Traffic offenses, in addition to fines, accumulate points on your driving history. These points serve as a measure of your driving behavior and can have significant consequences:

- **Insurance rates:** An increased tally of points on your driving record can result in higher insurance rates. Insurance companies view drivers with points as higher-risk clients, resulting in higher costs for coverage.

- **Driver's license suspension:** Accumulating too many points within a specific time frame can lead to your driver's license being suspended. This suspension lasts for a designated period, during which you cannot drive. Certain violations carry more severe penalties, such as license suspension or even revocation. Suspension means the loss of driving privileges for a designated amount of time. If your driver's license is revoked, it means permanent termination of your driver's license.

Understanding the Gravity

It's essential to recognize that traffic rule violations aren't mere inconveniences—they carry real and impactful consequences. Responsible driving is not only about avoiding fines but also about prioritizing safety, respecting the law, and contributing to the well-being of everyone on the road.

Fines, points, license suspension, and even imprisonment underscore the gravity of adhering to traffic laws. Being aware of the potential repercussions empowers you to make choices that prioritize safety and responsible driving.

Remember that each decision you make on the road has implications beyond the immediate moment. You play a significant role in creating a safer and more cooperative driving environment for all road users by upholding your driving responsibilities.

ROLE OF INSURANCE

Having car insurance is a legal requirement to drive in the state of California. It is a safety net that safeguards you, your passengers, and other road users from the financial and legal consequences of accidents. Adequate insurance coverage is essential to responsible driving, ensuring you're prepared for unforeseen circumstances and capable of fulfilling your obligations in case of accidents or injuries.

Different Types of Coverage

Understanding the various insurance coverage options is vital for making informed decisions about which policy to choose:

- **Liability coverage:** This type of insurance provides coverage if you're found at fault in an accident, including property damage and bodily injury expenses for the other party involved.
- **Collision coverage:** This type of insurance assists in covering the cost of repairing or replacing your vehicle in the event of a collision, regardless of fault.
- **Uninsured/Underinsured motorist coverage:** This type of auto insurance offers coverage in the event of an accident caused by an underinsured or uninsured driver.

Driving Without Insurance: Consequences for Driving Without Insurance in California

California law mandates that all drivers have at least the minimum required vehicle insurance coverage. Each driver needs to evaluate their unique financial situation, including net worth, to ensure they are insured adequately, protecting themselves and others on the road from the financial burdens arising from accidents and unforeseen circumstances.

Penalties for Driving Without Insurance

Driving without the minimum required insurance coverage in California carries a range of penalties designed to encourage compliance with the law and promote responsible driving behavior. Driving a vehicle without insurance can lead to fines. These fines can vary depending on the circumstances of the violation and whether it's a first-time offense or a repeat occurrence. Sometimes, driving without insurance can lead to the suspension of your driver's license. This suspension can create logistical challenges in your daily life as you lose all your driving privileges.

In certain circumstances, law enforcement may impound your vehicle if you're caught driving without insurance. This impoundment can result in additional expenses and inconvenience. If you're involved in an accident without insurance, you could be personally liable for covering the costs of physical damages, medical expenses, and legal fees for both your vehicle and the other party involved.

Impact on Future Insurance Rates

In addition to the immediate penalties, driving without insurance can impact your future insurance rates. Suppose you're able to obtain insurance after the violation. In that case, your premiums will likely increase significantly due to the higher perceived risk associated with your driving history.

The Responsible Choice

Driving without insurance violates the law and exposes you to substantial financial risks and potential legal consequences. It's essential to recognize that having insurance coverage is not just a legal requirement—it's a responsible decision that reflects your commitment to accountability on the road.

TYPES OF CAR INSURANCE AVAILABLE IN CALIFORNIA

A solid understanding of these insurance options is essential for every responsible driver. Each type of coverage serves a specific purpose, contributing to your safety and financial security on the road. Let's explore the six types available in California, according to the DMV (n.d.).

Personal Liability Coverage

Personal Liability Coverage, also known as Bodily Injury and Property Damage Liability, is a mandated insurance requirement in California. This coverage helps protect you financially if you're at fault in an accident that injures others or damages their property. It assists in covering the medical expenses, legal fees, and property repair costs for the other party involved.

Comprehensive Coverage

This type of insurance safeguards your vehicle against non-collision incidents such as theft, vandalism, natural disasters, and animal collisions. It offers financial assistance to repair or replace your vehicle in these scenarios.

Collision Coverage

This type of insurance policy provides coverage when your vehicle gets damaged in a collision, regardless of who's at fault. This coverage assists in covering the repair or replacement of your car in case it sustains damage in a collision.

Uninsured/Underinsured Motorist Coverage

Uninsured/Underinsured Motorist Coverage is valuable since it provides protection in the event of an accident caused by a driver without car insurance or with insufficient coverage to fully compensate for your injuries and damages. This coverage ensures you're not left bearing the financial burden due to the other person's lack of or insufficient insurance.

Medical Payments Coverage (Med Pay)

This type of policy includes coverage for medical expenses resulting from a car accident, regardless of fault. It encompasses hospital bills, doctor visits, and other medical costs for both you and your passengers.

Gap Coverage

Gap Coverage is relevant if you have a leased or financed vehicle. In the event of a total loss (when your car is considered a write-off due to a severe accident), Gap Coverage helps cover any difference between the loan balance and the value of your vehicle, preventing you from being financially responsible with the lien holder for the difference.

CHOOSING THE RIGHT COVERAGE

Selecting the appropriate types and amount of insurance coverage is critical to responsible driving. Your coverage should align with your needs, financial situation, and driving habits. Understanding the various types of coverage empowers you to make informed decisions prioritizing your safety, security, and compliance with the law.

REAL-LIFE ANECDOTE: CONSEQUENCES OF IRRESPONSIBILITY ON THE ROAD

In exploring driver responsibility and consequences, it's crucial to understand the real-life impact of irresponsibility behind the wheel. The story of State Representative Dan Wolgamott serves as a stark reminder of the severe repercussions that can arise from poor decision-making on the road (Faircloth, 2023).

In a recent incident, Representative Dan Wolgamott faced the consequences of a DWI (Driving While Intoxicated) arrest. This event serves as an illustration of the severe legal and personal ramifications that can result from driving under the influence.

Upon reflection, Representative Wolgamott publicly acknowledged his error and took full responsibility for his actions. His story underscores the importance of accountability and the recognition that even individuals in positions of authority are not exempt from the consequences of irresponsible behavior on the road.

Driving under the influence endangers the driver's life and threatens other road users and pedestrians. The incident is a stark reminder that adherence to traffic laws, responsible decision-making, and prioritizing the safety of oneself and others are fundamental aspects of being a responsible driver.

This story serves as a cautionary tale that resonates with all drivers. It emphasizes the need to recognize the gravity of poor choices on the road and the subsequent impact on one's life, reputation, and legal standing. By learning from real-life anecdotes like this, we gain valuable insights into the consequences of irresponsibility, promoting a culture of accountability, safety, and responsibility among drivers.

As we progress in our journey of becoming informed and responsible drivers, let's keep in mind that defensive driving techniques play a role in preventing accidents and violations. In the upcoming chapter, "Mastering Defensive Driving Techniques," we will delve into these strategies that empower you to anticipate, respond, and adapt to the unpredictable nature of the road.

Remember, responsible driving isn't just about following the rules—it's about embodying a mindset prioritizing safety, respect, and accountability.

INTERACTIVE QUIZ: TESTING YOUR UNDERSTANDING OF DRIVER RESPONSIBILITY AND CONSEQUENCES

Let's put your knowledge of driver responsibility and consequences to the test with some scenario-based questions. Consider each situation carefully and select the response that you believe reflects the responsible and safe course of action.

Scenario 1

You're driving down a busy street and notice the traffic light ahead has turned yellow. It's best to?

    a) Reduce speed and prepare to stop.
    b) Accelerate to clear the intersection before the light goes red.
    c) Continue at your current speed, regardless of the light.

Scenario 2

You entered a dedicated left turn lane but realize you are not at the street you wish to turn at. What's the best action to take?

a) Activate your turn signal and quickly move out of the turn lane.
b) Proceed to turn left and adjust your route accordingly to get to your destination.
c) Back up into the main road being careful not to cross the solid white line.

Scenario 3

You're driving on a highway and notice a police car on the shoulder with flashing lights. What should you do?

a) Slow down significantly to get a better look at what's happening.
b) Slow down and, if possible, move to the next lane to create a buffer between your vehicle and the police car.
c) Keep a steady speed and proceed with normal driving.

Scenario 4

You're at a party and have had a couple of alcoholic drinks. Your friends are recommending that you drive home. What is the responsible decision?

a) Accept their offer and drive home carefully.
b) Wait a bit longer and have a few more drinks before driving.
c) Politely decline and arrange for a sober driver, taxi, or rideshare.

Scenario 5

You're involved in a minor collision damaging another vehicle, and the other vehicle's owner is not present. What should you do?

a) Leave a note with your contact information.
b) Walk around and notify the first person you find of what happened and drive away.
c) Inspect the damage, and if it's minimal, leave without taking any action.

Scenario 6

You're about to exit a highway but realize you missed the exit. What should you do?

a) Continue driving until the next exit and find an alternate route.
b) Back up on the shoulder and take the missed exit.
c) Stop fully on the highway with your hazard lights on and wait for traffic to clear before reversing.

Your responses demonstrate your understanding of responsible driving practices and their potential consequences. Remember that responsible driving isn't just about following rules; it's about prioritizing safety, making ethical choices, and contributing to a secure and cooperative driving environment. Keep up the good work as you continue your journey to becoming a knowledgeable and responsible driver.

Answers
Scenario 1-a Scenario 2-b Scenario 3-b Scenario 4-c Scenario 5-a Scenario 6-a

7

MASTERING DEFENSIVE DRIVING TECHNIQUES

An ounce of prevention is worth a pound of cure.

— BENJAMIN FRANKLIN

In this case, defensive driving is that "ounce of prevention" when you're behind the wheel, potentially saving lives.

Defensive driving isn't just another phase of operating a vehicle—it's a mindset, a way of perceiving the road that empowers you to anticipate, adapt, and react adeptly to potential hazards. It goes beyond basic traffic rules and maneuvers; it's about being prepared for the unexpected and safeguarding yourself, your passengers, and other road users from harm.

Throughout this chapter, we'll explore a range of defensive driving techniques that will sharpen your instincts, enhance your situational awareness, and equip you to navigate even the trickiest of road scenarios confidently. From maintaining a safe following distance to recognizing and responding to aggressive driving behaviors, each technique you learn here will contribute to a comprehensive toolkit that can be the difference between an uneventful journey and a regrettable mishap.

But why is it of utmost importance to master defensive driving? It's more than just adhering to traffic laws—it's about taking personal responsibility for your actions on the road. By incorporating these techniques into your driving, you protect yourself and other drivers, fostering a safer driving environment for everyone on the road. This proactive approach reduces the likelihood of accidents, prevents injuries, and even helps to alleviate traffic congestion—making your everyday commutes smoother and more efficient.

By the time you've navigated through these pages, you'll have gained a rock-solid understanding of the concept of defensive driving, acquired a repertoire of techniques to avert accidents, and comprehended the invaluable benefits of adopting this proactive driving approach. The knowledge you'll gain here isn't just for acing your DMV exam—it's for a lifetime of safe and responsible driving. So, let's unravel the intricacies of defensive driving and empower you to handle the road's challenges with skill and confidence.

EXPLANATION OF DEFENSIVE DRIVING

As responsible drivers, we recognize that the road is an ever-changing environment, and potential dangers can arise at any moment. The philosophy of defensive driving revolves around minimizing risks and ensuring the safety of all road users through a combination of prudent actions and a heightened understanding of road dynamics.

A vital piece of defensive driving is anticipation. It entails surveying the road ahead to spot potential hazards in advance, providing you with sufficient time to respond appropriately. By maintaining a forward focus, you can spot upcoming intersections, pedestrians, and vehicles merging onto the road. Anticipation also extends to predicting the actions of other drivers, allowing you to adjust your speed and position to avoid potential conflicts. Remember, the more time you have to respond, the better your chances of preventing an accident.

Awareness is the glue that holds defensive driving together. Being fully aware of your surroundings means keeping an eye on what's happening in front of you and monitoring your mirrors and blind spots regularly. This comprehensive awareness helps you detect potential risks from all directions, enabling you to make split-second decisions if necessary. Cultivating this skill requires minimizing distractions inside the vehicle and staying attuned to the road's ever-changing conditions.

Then, we have preparation as your foundation for defensive driving. Part of defensive driving is positioning your vehicle in ways to maximize visibility and reduce blind spots. It also includes maintaining a safe following distance, allowing you ample time to brake or maneuver if the vehicle in front of you makes an unexpected move. Furthermore, proper hand placement on the steering wheel and keeping your foot poised over the brake pedal ensure you're ready to respond instantly to unforeseen circumstances.

The essence of defensive driving is demonstrated through your reactions to different situations on the road. Whether it's a sudden lane change by another driver, an approaching emergency vehicle, or adverse weather conditions, your ability to respond calmly and effectively can prevent potential accidents. Remember to prioritize safety over speed, signal your intentions early, and communicate your actions clearly to other drivers.

In mastering these fundamental principles of defensive driving, you're adopting a mindset that empowers you to take control of your driving environment, making it safer for yourself and others.

THE KEYS TO DEFENSIVE DRIVING

In our pursuit of mastering defensive driving techniques, we must equip ourselves with essential keys that unlock the door to safe, responsible, and proactive driving. These keys encapsulate the core principles that underscore the philosophy of defensive driving and serve as your guiding beacons on the road.

Think Safety First

Safety is more than just a priority; it's a way of thinking. Every decision you make behind the wheel should be rooted in the concern for your safety and the safety of others, adhering to traffic rules, restraining from risky maneuvers, and prioritizing caution over haste.

Be Aware of Your Surroundings—Pay Attention

Awareness is your sentinel against potential hazards. Keep your senses attuned to the road and its surroundings, scanning ahead, checking mirrors, and gauging the movement of vehicles around you. This acute attention lets you spot emerging threats early, giving you the time and space required to respond effectively. Remember, your awareness forms the bedrock of your defensive driving stance.

Do Not Depend on Other Drivers

Defensive driving rests on self-reliance. While you should anticipate the actions of other drivers, never rely solely on their adherence to rules or predictability. Maintain a safe amount of following distance, signal your intentions, and be ready for unexpected maneuvers. By assuming responsibility for your safety, you're better prepared to react if another driver behaves unexpectedly.

Follow the Three-Second Rule

The three-second rule is a minimum standard for maintaining a safe following distance. Pick a stationary object on the road ahead and count the seconds it takes for your vehicle to reach it after the vehicle in front of you passes it. This buffer gives you ample time to react if the car ahead slows down or stops suddenly. In adverse conditions, such as rain or low visibility, extend this time as much as necessary for safety.

Keep Your Speed Down

Speed directly impacts your reaction time and the severity of accidents. Adhering to speed limits is a legal requirement, but more importantly, adjust your speed to match road conditions. Driving within a safe speed range enhances your ability to perceive and react to potential dangers.

Have an Escape Route

Continuously think of an escape route. Visualize open spaces, shoulders, or adjacent lanes you can move into if a sudden hazard arises. This mental preparedness ensures that you're never boxed in and have room to maneuver away from potential collisions.

Separate Risks

Reduce risk by maintaining space around your vehicle. Avoid driving alongside other vehicles for extended periods, as you might be in the other driver's blind spot. If possible, maintain a buffer zone on all sides, reducing the chance of a collision if another driver makes an unexpected move.

Cut Out Distractions

Distractions compromise your ability to be a defensive driver. Keep your focus on the road, and avoid using your phone, adjusting the radio, or engaging in activities that take your attention away from driving. Eliminating distractions enhances your ability to anticipate and react to potential hazards.

By internalizing defensive driving principles and weaving them into your driving habits, you'll emerge as a driver who is aware of the road and actively shapes the road environment for safety.

TECHNIQUES TO PREVENT ACCIDENTS

As we venture deeper into defensive driving, we must equip ourselves with a comprehensive set of techniques that serve as shields against potential accidents. These techniques aren't mere suggestions; they're actionable strategies that, when practiced diligently, create a robust layer of safety around your driving experience.

Maintaining a Safe Distance

- **Step 1**: Adhere to the three-second rule for following distance and increase it during adverse weather conditions or when driving behind larger vehicles.
- **Scenario:** Picture the car in front of you abruptly hitting its brakes. Or you are following a pickup truck that is heavily loaded, and suddenly, some of the items in the bed of the pickup fly off into the road in front of you. Having a safe distance allows you the time needed to brake smoothly and avoid a collision.

Scanning the Road

- **Step 1:** Scan the road ahead, checking mirrors every five to eight seconds.
- **Scenario:** By actively observing your surroundings, you're prepared to react if a car suddenly merges into your lane without signaling.

Adapting to Weather Conditions

- **Step 1:** Reduce speed and increase your following distance to more than three seconds in rain, snow, or fog.
- **Scenario:** Driving slower and maintaining extra space allows you to account for reduced visibility and longer braking distances.

Respecting Other Drivers

- **Step 1:** Yield the right of way as required by traffic laws.
- **Scenario:** When approaching a four-way stop, ensure you let the driver who arrived first proceed, promoting orderly traffic flow and preventing confusion. Remember that in the event of a tie, the vehicle positioned to the right gets the right of way.

Avoid Distractions

Minimize activities that divert your attention from the road, such as texting, talking on the phone, or fiddling with the radio. Your focus should remain on driving and observing your surroundings.

Stay Alert

Fatigue and drowsiness diminish your reaction time. Get adequate rest before beginning your journey and take breaks if driving for extended periods.

Look Ahead Down the Road

Constantly scanning the road ahead helps you anticipate potential obstacles or slowdowns, allowing you to react smoothly.

Responding to Other Drivers

Remain patient and courteous when interacting with other drivers. If another driver makes a mistake, avoid confrontations and give them space.

Observe the Rules of Right-Of-Way

Understanding and adhering to right-of-way rules prevents confusion and reduces the risk of collisions at intersections or when merging. An example is three-way intersections without a stop from either of the three directions; in this type of intersection, the right of way goes to pedestrians or vehicles in the "through" street.

Anticipate Other Drivers' Reactions

Predict how other drivers might behave and adjust your driving accordingly. Unfortunately, some drivers will focus on getting to a destination the quickest way possible and disregard the safety of others, which opens the door to risk-taking by drivers. Your anticipation of these risks by other drivers prepares you for sudden lane changes, unexpected stops, or other abrupt actions.

Don't Resort to Road Rage

Maintain your composure in frustrating situations. Aggressive behavior only escalates tension and increases the chances of verbal or physical altercations and accidents.

Control Your Speed

Adjust your speed based on road conditions. Remember, driving at a slower speed allows for better reaction times.

Let Other Drivers Know What You're Doing

Signal your intentions early by using turn signals for lane changes, upcoming turns at corners, turning into driveways, or a business parking lot. Move over to the rightmost part of the lane, including entering the bike lane for right turns. Be sure to avoid slowing down late, as this increases your chances of being hit from behind. Effective communication fosters a more seamless traffic flow, thereby improving safety.

HANDLING DANGEROUS SITUATIONS

It's essential to acknowledge that the road isn't always a predictable and serene environment. There are times when unexpected obstacles and challenging interactions arise. You must remain calm to make the best split-second decisions possible, which is the difference between avoiding a collision or making it a minor collision rather than a major one if the crash is unavoidable.

On-Road Obstacles

Scenario: You're driving along an unfamiliar route, and there are high gusts of wind. Suddenly, a large tree branch falls onto the road.

- **Step 1:** Maintain a safe following distance greater than three seconds due to the high wind; this gives you ample time to react to unforeseen obstacles.
- **Step 2:** Keep scanning ahead, noting potential hazards like debris, animals, or stalled vehicles.
- **Step 3:** When confronted with this obstacle, resist the urge to swerve abruptly. Instead, brake smoothly and steer around gradually without losing control.

These techniques prepare you to navigate unexpected obstacles without jeopardizing your safety or the safety of others.

Navigating Aggressive Drivers

One of the most challenging scenarios you may encounter is interacting with aggressive drivers. These individuals can turn a routine commute into a tense situation, testing your patience and skills.

Deal With Patience

- **Step 1:** Stay calm and composed. Do not allow another driver's aggression to affect your emotional state.
- **Step 2:** Avoid aggressive gestures, shouting matches, or retaliating. These behaviors only escalate the situation.

Patience and calmness are your allies in diffusing tense situations and upholding the principles of defensive driving.

Drive Defensively

- **Step 1:** Focus on your driving but stay vigilant by scanning. Keep a safe following distance and obey traffic rules.

- **Step 2:** Avoid any behavior that might provoke or worsen the situation. Maintain a steady speed and predictable movements.

Defensive driving involves prioritizing safety and responsibility, regardless of the behavior of other drivers.

Fighting Back and Overcoming Emotional Distress

- **Step 1:** Refrain from taking the actions of aggressive drivers personally. Their behavior often stems from unrelated factors.
- **Step 2:** Focus on your well-being and safety, as your goal is to arrive at your destination safely.

Overcoming emotional distress empowers you to stay in control and make rational decisions on the road.

Politely Deal With Other Drivers

- **Step 1:** If confronted by another driver, avoid making eye contact or engaging in arguments.
- **Step 2:** If another driver attempts to engage you, remain polite but noncommittal. Do not engage in verbal disputes.
- **Step 3:** If the other driver continues to be a threat, dial 911 to get assistance from law enforcement and drive to the nearest police station or a public place, reducing the chances of the situation escalating further.

Maintaining your composure and civility prevents the situation from escalating and ensures your safety.

Maintain a Distance

- **Step 1:** Keep a safe following distance from aggressive drivers, allowing you space to react to their sudden maneuvers.

- **Step 2:** If an aggressive driver tailgates you, maintain your speed and avoid speeding up to appease them.

Maintaining a safe distance is crucial in avoiding collisions and preventing the aggressive behavior of others from affecting your driving.

DEALING WITH AGGRESSIVE DRIVERS: SCENARIOS

Scenario 1: An Impatient Driver Behind You is Tailgating and Honking Incessantly.

- **Step 1:** Avoid engaging in aggressive behavior or retaliating. Stay focused on your driving.
- **Step 2:** Keep a steady speed and signal your intention to change lanes.

In this case, you retain control over the situation, ensuring your safety and that of other road users.

Scenario 2: Another Driver Reacts Aggressively to a Driving Error You've Made, Escalating the Situation Into a Road Rage Incident.

- **Step 1:** It's best to avoid eye contact or interacting with an irate driver. Concentrate on safe and responsible driving.
- **Step 2:** If the situation worsens, call law enforcement or drive to a public area if you feel threatened.
- **Step 3:** Do not let road rage affect your emotions or driving behavior. Stay composed and adhere to the principles of defensive driving.

This approach helps you control your reactions, mitigating potential risks associated with road rage incidents.

Navigating aggressive drivers requires a delicate balance of patience, composure, and defensive driving skills. Employing these strategies provides you with the best opportunity to prevent a road rage incident.

BENEFITS OF DEFENSIVE DRIVING

The advantages extend far beyond merely passing your DMV exam. Embracing defensive driving principles can significantly enhance your driving experience, making you a safer, more responsible and confident driver.

Reduces Driving Risks

Defensive driving is synonymous with risk reduction. By anticipating potential hazards and acting pre-emptively, you significantly decrease the likelihood of accidents or collisions. Your ability to perceive dangerous situations beforehand empowers you to make informed decisions, prioritizing safety and preventing potentially harmful scenarios from unfolding.

Improves Your Driving Skills

Mastering defensive driving techniques sharpens your driving skills across the board. You become more attuned to road conditions, traffic patterns, and the behavior of other drivers; this heightened awareness translates to improved control over your vehicle, smoother maneuvering, and enhanced decision-making skills while on the road.

Accident-Free Techniques

The core philosophy of defensive driving revolves around minimizing risks and preventing accidents. You actively engage in practices that contribute to accident prevention by consistently implementing defensive driving techniques; this means fewer near misses and a reduced likelihood of collisions.

Defensive driving is, at its heart, a proactive safety measure. By keeping a safe following distance, scanning the road ahead, and adhering to traffic rules, you're positioning yourself for maximum protection in unexpected events; this added safety layer ensures you're well-prepared to handle sudden challenges without compromising your well-being.

No Violation Charges

Defensive driving techniques align with traffic laws and regulations; driving defensively minimizes the chances of receiving traffic citations, thus keeping your driving record clean and ensuring your auto insurance rates stay as low as possible.

Less Maintenance

Defensive driving practices extend the lifespan of your vehicle. You reduce wear and tear on your vehicle's components by avoiding sudden stops, maintaining a safe distance, and driving smoothly. The result is fewer repairs, which saves you money and a longer-lasting vehicle.

Mitigating Traffic Congestion

Defensive driving isn't just about reacting to immediate dangers; it's about preventing the domino effect of accidents that can cascade into massive traffic congestion. By practicing anticipatory and cautious driving, you contribute to the uninterrupted flow of traffic, minimizing delays and ensuring that the roadways remain efficient.

Reducing Economic Impact

Accidents don't just take a physical and emotional toll—they also carry a significant economic burden. Defensive driving mitigates this impact by reducing the occurrence of accidents and their subsequent costs, including medical expenses, property damage, and increased auto insurance rates.

Enhancing Personal Confidence

Mastering defensive driving techniques fosters a sense of confidence and empowerment.

By embracing defensive driving principles like anticipation, awareness, and preparedness, you embody the ethos of a responsible driver, creating a safer, more harmonious road environment for everyone. This chapter isn't just about passing your DMV exam—it's about becoming a confident, responsible driver. You've discovered how maintaining a safe following distance, scanning the road, adapting to weather conditions, and respecting other drivers can all contribute to a safer driving experience.

As we conclude this chapter, it's important to reflect on the wealth of knowledge you've acquired. From understanding the philosophy of defensive driving to delving into specific techniques, you've now equipped yourself with a powerful set of tools that will shape your driving journey in meaningful ways.

By internalizing the principles of anticipation, awareness, and preparedness, you've embraced a proactive approach to driving—one that prioritizes safety, responsibility, and respect for fellow road users. You've discovered how maintaining a safe following distance, scanning the road, adapting to weather conditions, and respecting other drivers can all contribute to a safer driving experience.

But knowledge alone is not enough; true mastery comes from application. Now is the time to take the ideas presented in this chapter and put them into action. As you embark on your driving journey, remember the importance of patience, staying alert, and maintaining distance from other vehicles. By applying these techniques consistently, you're not just preparing for your DMV exam; you're actively becoming a safer and more confident driver.

Now that you've learned defensive driving techniques and how they can keep you safe on the road, it's time to bring together all that knowledge for your final preparation. In the next chapter, "Extra Preparation for Your Test," we'll provide additional resources and strategies to ensure you're fully prepared and confident for your exam. This comprehensive approach will empower you to navigate the exam with ease and showcase the skills you've acquired throughout this handbook.

As you move forward, remember that defensive driving is more than just a set of techniques—it's a mindset that shapes your behavior behind the wheel. By integrating these principles into your driving routine, you're not only safeguarding yourself but also contributing to a safer road environment for all. Your journey toward becoming a responsible, proactive, and skilled driver is well underway, and the next chapter will guide you closer to your goal of success on the road and in the DMV exam.

DECISION-MAKING GAME

With a decision-making game, let's test your newfound knowledge of defensive driving techniques. This game will present you with a series of road scenarios, each with multiple choices. Your task is to choose the response that best aligns with the principles of defensive driving.

Scenario 1: Erratically Driving Vehicle

You're driving on a busy highway, and a car ahead of you is driving erratically. What's the best defensive driving response?

a) Increase the following distance and stay behind the erratically driving car.
b) Brake suddenly to assure you stay as far as possible.
c) Increase your speed to pass the car driving erratically; it's safer to be in front.
d) Change lanes and drive next to the erratically driving car.

Scenario 2: Actively Scan While You Drive

While driving through a residential area, a child suddenly runs out onto the road chasing a ball. What's the best defensive driving response?

a) Honk loudly and continue driving at your current speed.
b) Immediately swerve sharply to avoid hitting the child.
c) Brake as gently as possible while still assuring you do not hit the child, come to a controlled stop, and honk to alert the child.
d) Accelerate to quickly pass the child before they reach your lane.

Scenario 3: Unpredictable Merge

You're on the rightmost lane on a freeway, and the driver in the merging lane seems unaware of your presence. What's the best defensive driving response?

a) Speed up to stay ahead of them and assert your position.
b) If it is safe, change lanes or adjust your speed accordingly to allow room for the other driver to merge without colliding with you.
c) Maintain your speed and force them to yield to you.
d) Honk loudly to get their attention and maintain your speed.

Scenario 4: Unpredictable Hazard

You're driving on a busy city street, and the car in front of you suddenly slams on its brakes for an object on the road. What's the best defensive driving response?

a) Swerve into the next lane to avoid rear-ending the car.
b) Slam on your brakes as well to stop in time, even if it means skidding.

c) Keep an adequate following distance and brake smoothly to come to a controlled stop.

d) Honk loudly to express your frustration with the sudden stop.

Scenario 5: Blind Intersection

You are at a one-way stop, and overgrown bushes obstruct your view; you can't see if any vehicles are coming from the side street. What's the best defensive driving response?

a) Quickly accelerate to cross the intersection before any cars approach.

b) Stop behind the limit line, then inch forward slowly until you get a view past the bushes and proceed once you confirm it is safe to do so.

c) Honk continuously to alert any approaching vehicles of your presence.

d) Stop a few feet past the stop line to get a better view of the side street.

Scenario 6: Honking From Another Driver

While attempting to merge onto a highway, another driver honks angrily at you for trying to merge at a slower speed. What's the best defensive driving response?

a) Adjust your speed accordingly for your safety and that of the other driver and determine if it is safer to merge behind the other driver instead of trying to merge ahead.

b) Ignore them and continue merging at your own pace.

c) Speed up abruptly to match their speed and assert your presence.

d) Use your brakes abruptly to teach them a valuable lesson.

Scenario 7: Tailgating Challenge

You notice a car tailgating closely behind you, even though you're already driving at the speed limit. What's the best defensive driving response?

a) Tap your brakes to warn them about their following distance.
b) Do a sudden slow-down.
c) When safe, make a lane change.
d) Speed up to see if they'll back off and give you more room.

Remember, your choices on the road are essential in ensuring the safety of yourself and others. As you progress in your journey, reflect on the scenarios and responses provided. Let your commitment to defensive driving guide your actions in real-world situations.

Answers
Scenario 1: a) Scenario 2: c) Scenario 3: b) Scenario 4: c)
Scenario 5: b) Scenario 6: a) Scenario 7: c)

8

HELPFUL RESOURCES

An investment in knowledge pays the best interest.

— BENJAMIN FRANKLIN

Congratulations on making your way through the *California DMV Exam Handbook*! By now, you've absorbed a wealth of knowledge about the rules of the road, defensive driving practices, and the responsibilities of obtaining a learner's permit. But your learning journey doesn't end with the test: It's just the beginning of a lifelong commitment to safe and responsible driving.

Here, you will find a careful list of materials, websites, and organizations that offer a wealth of information on various aspects of driving, traffic regulations, and road safety. Whether you're a novice driver looking to build confidence or an experienced motorist seeking to stay updated with the latest changes in California's driving laws, these resources will prove invaluable.

So, as you approach the end of this handbook, remember that the road to becoming a proficient driver is an ongoing journey. The resources in this chapter will serve as your trusted companions, guiding you toward a safer and more confident driving experience. Embrace them, learn from them, and drive responsibly to protect yourself and those around you. After all, safe driving is a commitment, not just a skill, and it begins with the knowledge and resources at your disposal.

WEBSITES, APPS, AND BOOKS

In your journey to becoming an informed driver in California, it's crucial to harness the power of various resources beyond the confines of this handbook. These include official websites, mobile apps, and official vehicle code books to enhance your understanding of road rules, driving laws, and safety practices. Additionally, we'll discuss the potential benefits of utilizing local library resources.

DMV California (Official Website)

https://www.dmv.ca.gov/

The California Department of Motor Vehicles (DMV) maintains an official website that serves as a treasure trove of information. Here, you'll find comprehensive details on driver's licensing, vehicle registration, traffic laws, and anything related to vehicle matters, and is an excellent resource for exam preparation.

Driving-Tests.org

https://driving-tests.org/

Driving-Tests.org is a valuable platform offering a collection of practice exams tailored to California's DMV requirements. Their user-friendly app is designed to help you prepare thoroughly for the DMV written test. You can access a variety of practice questions and simulations to boost your confidence.

Driving Books

Several reputable books are dedicated to safe driving practices and preparing for the DMV exam, like the *California Driver Handbook* (the official DMV handbook), which provides comprehensive insights into California's driving laws, road signs, and safe driving tips. It can serve as a valuable reference material as you embark on your journey to becoming a responsible driver.

To ensure that you derive the maximum benefit from these resources, it's important to approach your learning journey with a structured and proactive mindset.

UTILIZING RESOURCES

To ensure you benefit from these resources, approach your learning journey with a structured and proactive mindset.

Subscribe to Newsletters

Stay informed about changes in California driving laws and regulations by subscribing to newsletters from trusted sources. The DMV's official website often provides updates and newsletters to help you stay current.

Participate in Online Forums

Engage with the driving community by joining online forums or discussion boards dedicated to driving in California. These platforms can be valuable for asking questions, sharing experiences, and learning from other drivers.

Stay Up to Date

Driving laws and regulations may change over time. Make it a habit to check for updates on the DMV's website and other trusted sources. Keeping your knowledge current is essential, even after passing your initial exam.

Seek Guidance When Needed

Feel free to seek advice from a driving instructor, mentor, or experienced driver if you encounter challenging concepts or have questions. Getting clarification on doubts can prevent misunderstandings down the road.

Stay Committed to Safe Driving

Remember that the ultimate goal of all this learning is to become a safe and responsible driver. Apply what you've learned not just during your exam but in your everyday driving experiences.

These resources are invaluable tools, and by using them effectively, you'll not only pass the test but also become a more knowledgeable and confident driver on California's roads.

Obtaining Your Driver's License

Congratulations! You have now attained your learner's permit, allowing you to practice driving, but one crucial step remains the driving test. You must return to the DMV to take the practical driving test. If you are 18 or older, you can take the exam as soon as you feel ready. For minors, there is a 6-month wait period before being eligible to take the behind-the-wheel test; minors must also attain a 6-hour completion certificate from a certified driving school. During this examination, the examiner will assess your driving skills to ensure you can safely navigate California's roads. Upon passing the driving test, you will receive a full-fledged driver's license from the DMV.

Updating Your Insurance

With the attainment of your driver's license, it's essential to consider your financial responsibility as a driver. California requires all drivers to have auto insurance coverage. It's your responsibility to obtain an insurance policy that meets the minimum requirements set by the state. Contact local insurance providers to obtain the necessary coverage and ensure you comply with California's insurance laws.

Vehicle Registration Requirements

Additionally, as a vehicle owner in California, you'll need to ensure that your vehicle's registration is current. Registering your vehicle involves providing the DMV with essential information, such as its year, make, and vehicle identification number (VIN). After the initial vehicle registration, there will be annual renewal fees.

For a detailed guide on vehicle registration requirements and how to complete the process, consider referring to the official DMV resources or seeking assistance from your local DMV office.

In-Car Driving Lessons

You will need to demonstrate complete vehicle control to pass the behind-the-wheel test. Keep in mind that the learner's permit is only valid for driving when accompanied by a licensed driver aged 25 or older. Additionally, all minors are required to complete 6 hours of behind-the-wheel training before becoming eligible to take the behind-the-wheel test. The DMV also recommends minors do 50 hours of practice outside the 6 hours with the driving school, with 10 of those hours being at night. While not required for adult learners, professional driving lessons enhance learning and assist in developing defensive driving techniques.

SAFE DRIVING POST-LICENSE: A LIFELONG COMMITMENT TO RESPONSIBLE DRIVING

It's important to know that the road to becoming a safe driver doesn't conclude with the issuance of your license; it is an enduring commitment. In this section, we will emphasize the critical importance of continuing safe driving habits, including defensive driving, abstaining from alcohol while driving, and adhering to speed limits.

Defensive Driving

Remember that adopting a defensive driving mindset is one of the fundamental principles of safe driving. This approach means staying alert and prepared for the unexpected on the road. Defensive drivers anticipate possible hazards, keep a safe following distance, and stay watchful of the behaviors of other road users.

Say No to Drinking and Driving

It should go without saying, but we must emphasize the importance of never getting behind the wheel after consuming alcohol. Driving under the influence poses an enormous risk to your safety and others on the road. Always assign a designated driver or utilize alternative transportation if you've consumed alcohol. The consequences of driving under the influence are both legally and morally severe.

Respect Speed Limits

Speed limits are not random figures; they are established to guarantee safe travel on the road. Excessive speed diminishes reaction time and augments the severity of accidents. It is crucial to consistently abide by posted speed limits, particularly in inclement weather or regions with substantial pedestrian traffic.

Benefits of Safe Driving Rewards

Safe driving extends beyond merely preventing accidents; it brings tangible rewards. You can save on insurance premiums by maintaining a clean driving record and practicing responsible driving habits. Safe drivers are also less likely to incur fines or penalties, contributing to financial savings.

Passing the written exam is a significant milestone. Still, it marks the beginning of your journey as a licensed driver in California. Remember to schedule your driving test, obtain auto insurance, and ensure your vehicle is properly registered. Embrace the responsibility of safe and responsible driving and consider additional training through in-car lessons to enhance your skills. As you embark on this new chapter, continue to educate yourself on California's driving laws and regulations, and always prioritize safety.

As we conclude this chapter, we encourage you to put the ideas presented here into action.

Keep in mind that nobody has the right to drive; it's a privilege; it's a responsibility that impacts your safety and the safety of others. With the knowledge and resources you've acquired, you are now well-prepared to take on this responsibility with confidence and diligence. Safe travels and may your journey as a responsible driver always be joyful, courteous, and safe.

DISCLAIMER

As we begin the practice exams, it is essential to understand that it would be virtually impossible for this book to cover every possible scenario or California driving law you might encounter in the DMV knowledge test.

We encourage you to use this book in conjunction with the Official California Vehicle Code, which is available through the California DMV's official website or at local DMV offices. The vehicle code contains the most detailed and comprehensive information on California's traffic laws and regulations, and it should be consulted whenever you have questions or encounter specific scenarios not covered in this handbook.

Remember, the DMV exam is designed to ensure that you thoroughly understand California's driving laws and can apply them safely on the road. Now, let's begin with the questions.

9

EXTRA PREPARATION FOR YOUR TEST

Success depends upon previous preparation, and without such preparation, there is sure to be failure.

— CONFUCIUS

From wise Confucius, these words ring especially true in your journey toward obtaining your California driver's license. The culmination of all your learning and practice is just around the corner. In this chapter, we will ensure that you're fully equipped to pass the California DMV exam easily.

The previous chapters laid a solid foundation of knowledge and skills necessary for safe and responsible driving. As the test day looms, it's time to focus on those crucial extra steps that can elevate your preparation to the next level.

We'll delve into proven strategies that make the most of your remaining preparation time.

Feeling a surge of nerves is typical before a significant event like the DMV exam. However, the key is to channel that nervous energy into positive outcomes. This section will explore relaxation techniques, mindfulness practices, and mental exercises to avoid stress and anxiety. By the time you step into the exam room, you'll be armed with the tools to maintain a clear and focused mind.

Simulating the test is one of the most effective ways to assess your readiness. By applying your knowledge and skills in this simulated scenario, you'll identify areas for improvement and build the confidence needed to excel on test day.

As you work through this chapter, you'll find your self-assurance growing. Remember, you've put in the effort, honed your skills, and gained the necessary knowledge. It's time to trust in your preparation.

LAST-MINUTE TIPS AND TECHNIQUES

As the big day approaches, it's time to fine-tune your skills and gather the last-minute tips and techniques that can make all the difference.

Revisiting Crucial Traffic Rules and Road Signs

Before you take the test, take some time to brush up on essential traffic rules and road signs. Review the right-of-way rules, speed limits, and various road signs. This quick review will reinforce your knowledge and boost your confidence when taking the test.

A Good Night's Sleep: Your Secret Weapon

Sleep is your ultimate ally. Make sure to get a solid night's rest before the test day. A well-rested mind is sharper and more focused, allowing you to make split-second decisions and react appropriately to different driving situations. Adequate sleep enhances your cognitive abilities and keeps anxiety at bay.

Fueling Your Body With a Healthy Meal

On the morning of your test, opt for a balanced meal to provide sustained energy. Avoid heavy, greasy foods that might leave you feeling sluggish. A well-fueled body contributes to clearer thinking and increased alertness.

Arriving Early: Set the Tone for Success

Ensure you have ample time for any unexpected delays, which helps calm your nerves. When you're not rushing, you can take a moment to mentally prepare, review your notes, and visualize your success.

TEST TIPS FOR A SUCCESSFUL KNOWLEDGE TEST

Remember, success on the driving test requires practical skills, knowledge, and a composed demeanor. Here are some additional tips that can guide you toward a successful outcome:

- **DMV practice tests:** Familiarize yourself with the DMV practice tests in this book and on the DMV website. They offer valuable insights into the format and types of questions you might encounter.
- **Timing matters:** Wait to take the test until you're truly ready. Ensure you've honed your skills and feel confident in your abilities.

As you prepare for your California DMV exam, remember that success results from your dedication, practice, and determination. Approach the test with a clear mind and the knowledge you've put in the effort necessary to pass the exam easily. Trust in your abilities, stay composed, and let your hard work shine through.

Ensure You Have All Necessary Documents

Double-check that you have all the required documents before arriving to take the test. Being well-prepared in this regard reflects your responsibility as a future driver.

MANAGING EXAM STRESS

The knowledge test is a significant milestone, and while a touch of anxiety is typical, managing stress effectively can make a world of difference in your performance. That's why finding ways to channel your nervousness constructively is essential. Let's explore some proven techniques to manage exam stress.

Deep Breathing Exercises

When stress starts to rise, take a moment to focus on your breathing. Inhale deeply through your nose, hold for a count of four, and then slowly exhale through your mouth. This simple technique calms your nervous system and clears your mind.

Visualization Techniques

Picture yourself confidently understanding and correctly answering all the exam questions. Visualization not only boosts your confidence but also preps your mind for success.

Positive Affirmations

Replace self-doubt with positive self-talk. Remind yourself of your capabilities and achievements. Affirmations like "I am prepared and confident" can profoundly impact your mindset.

The Power of a Positive Mindset

Approaching your permit test with a positive mindset is a game-changer. It's not just about thinking positively but about cultivating a mental environment supporting your success. Here are the top ways to infuse positivity into your test day:

- **Tell yourself you're ready:** Remember the countless hours invested in learning and practice. Trust in your preparation and reassure yourself that you're well-equipped to handle the test.
- **Keep it a secret:** Sharing your test day plans with too many people can amplify stress. Keep your circle small and share only with those who provide encouragement and support.
- **Don't skip meals:** A balanced meal fuels your body and mind. Don't skip meals, as it can lead to energy crashes and increased stress. Choose nutrient-rich options that provide sustained energy throughout the day.
- **Pretend it's a mock:** Approach the test as if it were a mock exam. This mindset shift can ease the pressure and allow you to showcase your skills more naturally.

Stay Off the Caffeine

Excess caffeine can intensify nervousness and restlessness. Opt for calming herbal teas instead.

As you approach your California DMV exam, remember that managing stress is integral to your preparation. Implement these strategies and think positively to enhance your performance and give you a more enjoyable test experience.

NAVIGATING TEST DAY WITH EASE: AVOIDING STRESS FOR DRIVING SUCCESS

The day of your California DMV permit test has arrived, and the mix of excitement and apprehension is typical; however, it's crucial to keep stress at bay for this life-altering examination.

Organize Your Time

Time management is a valuable skill, even on test days. Plan your morning routine in a way that allows you to comfortably get ready without rushing. Allocate sufficient time for meals, dressing, and travel. By keeping a steady pace, you'll enter the test center with a composed and relaxed demeanor.

Breathe

Before you step into the examination area, pause for a moment and Inhale deeply through your nose, hold for a count of four, and then slowly exhale through your mouth. (Greenshield, 2019). This calming breath helps ease nervous tension and centers your focus. Remember that you've prepared diligently and are ready to demonstrate your skills.

Be Confident

Incorporating these stress-relieving techniques into your test day routine allows you to create a more positive and composed experience. Remember, stress is a natural response to significant events, but rest easy knowing you are armed with ways to manage it effectively. Approach your California DMV permit test with confidence, clarity, and the knowledge you've put in the effort to be well-prepared.

Driving is not just about skill; it's also about maintaining a calm and focused mindset. As you embark on this leg of your journey to becoming a licensed driver, remember these strategies.

MOCK DMV TEST

Congratulations on reaching this stage of your journey to becoming a licensed driver in California. To help you gauge your readiness for the upcoming DMV driving test, we've prepared a comprehensive mock test. This test covers a range of topics, including rules of the road, road signs, and defensive driving techniques. Remember, the more you practice, the more confident and prepared you'll be on test day.

The questions provided here are a sample of the types of questions you may encounter on the California DMV permit test. The actual test may vary in content and format. Your dedication to practice and preparation is key to achieving success. Best of luck as you move closer to your goal of becoming a licensed driver!

Please select the correct answer for each question.

1. Which of these is true regarding maximum speed limits in California?

    a. You may legally drive 10 to 15 miles per hour above the speed limit on any freeway.
    b. You may legally drive 5 to 10 miles above the speed limit on any city street.
    c. You may not legally drive above the maximum limit for any reason.
    d. It is not applicable when you are driving with the flow of traffic.

2. It is _____ to drive at night with only one functioning headlight?

    a. Illegal
    b. Unsafe
    c. Both of the above
    d. None of the above

3. When passing another vehicle, when is it safe to merge back into your lane?

    a. When you hear the other vehicle's horn
    b. When the vehicle is no longer visible in your side mirror
    c. Once you are at least one car length ahead of the vehicle
    d. When you can see the vehicle's headlights in your rearview mirror

4. you give consent to take a chemical test:

    a. Only if you are involved in an accident
    b. Whenever you drive in California
    c. Only if an officer suspects you of being under the influence
    d. Only if you refuse a breathalyzer test

5. The safest way to back up (go in reverse) is

a. Do it quickly before anyone gets to park behind you
b. Rely solely on a backup camera if the vehicle is equipped with one
c. Looking solely on your rearview mirror
d. Look out the rear window looking over your right shoulder and glancing to the sides

6. What is the safest practice when driving on a poorly lit street at night?

a. Use your high beams continuously
b. Follow the vehicle ahead closely to improve your visibility
c. Drive slow enough to stop within the distance illuminated by your headlights
d. Maintain the posted speed limit despite the low visibility

7. When approaching a roundabout, you should

a. Speed up to merge with traffic
b. Slow down and yield to traffic in the circle
c. Come to a complete stop
d. Swerve around the vehicles already in the circle

8. When switching lanes on the freeway, how long should you signal?

a. 7 seconds
b. 3 seconds
c. 10 seconds
d. 5 seconds

9. Choose the correct statement in regard to a "passing lane":

   a. Drivers must not exceed the maximum speed limit to pass

   b. Its purpose is to ease the backlog in rural one-lane roads

   c. Drivers going slower are to move to the right to allow other drivers to pass using the passing lane

   d. All of the above

10. If your cell phone rings while you're driving, the best course of action is to:

   a. Let the call go to voice mail

   b. Slow down to safely answer the call

   c. Answer it at once to avoid distractions down the road

   d. Both A and B

11. Drivers shall not exceed _____ while driving through a school zone in which children are present:

   a. 45 mph

   b. 30 mph

   c. 25 mph

   d. 10 mph

12. To complete a merge, you must

   a. Lower your window and point straight down

   b. Stop to make sure it is safe to proceed

   c. Activate your hazard lights

   d. Perform the maneuver like a lane change using the turn signal, looking at the side mirror, and looking over your shoulder

13. When there are two lanes moving in your direction, and you're in the left lane with vehicles frequently passing you on the right, the best practice is to:

    a. Increase your speed to keep up with traffic
    b. Move to the right lane when it's safe
    c. Continue driving in the left lane
    d. Honk to signal other drivers to slow down

14. When attempting to pass a slower vehicle on a two-lane road with traffic moving in opposite directions, you must:

    a. Honk to signal the vehicle to move over
    b. Use the lane for oncoming traffic
    c. Pass on the right shoulder
    d. Use hand signals for oncoming traffic to see you are passing

15. Which of these is the most dangerous to your steering control?

    a. Solid ice on the road
    b. Gently falling snow
    c. Water runoff from broken sprinklers
    d. Any surface if the temperature is above 95 degrees

16. You should watch for bicyclists in lanes used by motorists because:

    a. Bicyclists are allowed to share the road with motor vehicles
    b. They often ride faster than vehicles
    c. They are required to stay in the center of the lane
    d. They always have the right of way over motor vehicles

17. What does a red octagonal sign mean?

a. Stop
b. Yield
c. Merge
d. Slow down

18. You miss and drive past your freeway exit, you should

a. Continue driving and find an alternate route
b. Make a U-turn on the freeway
c. Back up on the freeway to the exit
d. Stop and wait for help

19. Leaving an animal on the roadway could lead to:

a. Six months in jail
b. A fine up to $1000
c. A minor fine with no further consequences
d. Both A and B

20. What is the penalty for receiving a second citation within 3 years for using a handheld cell phone while driving in California?

a. A warning
b. A fine of $20
c. A fine and a point against your driving record
d. None of the above

21. When merging onto a freeway, you should:

a. Come to a complete stop before entering the freeway
b. Speed up and force your way into traffic
c. Adjust your speed to match the flow and look for a gap to merge smoothly into traffic

d. Signal and move in at least 10 miles slower than traffic

22. You are driving on a two-lane road with a solid yellow line on your side. Can you pass other vehicles?

a. Yes, if the vehicle in front of you is going too slow
b. Yes, if you use your turn signal
c. No, passing is not allowed
d. Yes, if you can see ahead clearly

23. When a traffic signal turns green, you should

a. Accelerate as quickly as possible
b. Yield the right-of-way to pedestrians and vehicles still in the intersection
c. Honk your horn to alert other drivers
d. Change lanes immediately

24. You must use your headlights

a. After 5 in the evening
b. Half an hour before sunrise and half an hour after sunset
c. When driving in heavy traffic
d. When driving on the freeway

25. When is it best for you to yield your legal right of way?

a. Only when the other driver is speeding
b. If it helps prevent a collision
c. Only at intersections
d. When your vehicle is to the left

26. If crossing an intersection and an emergency vehicle approaches with flashing lights, it's best to:

  a. Stop immediately in the intersection
  b. Speed up to clear the intersection as quickly as possible
  c. Continue through the intersection, then pull over to the right and stop
  d. Ignore the emergency vehicle and proceed normally

27. In regard to driving, what does the "Three-Second Rule" mean?

  a. You should follow at least three seconds behind the vehicle in front of you
  b. You should follow at least three car lengths behind the vehicle in front of you
  c. You should follow at least three minutes behind the vehicle in front of you
  d. You should follow at least three feet behind the vehicle in front of you

28. What should you do if you experience a tire blowout while driving?

  a. Slam on the brakes
  b. Steer sharply to the side of the road
  c. Hold the steering wheel firmly and gradually slow down
  d. Shift into neutral and coast to a stop

29. When executing a right turn with a red light, you are required to

  a. Come to a complete stop and yield the right-of-way to all other traffic
  b. Slow down, but you can turn without stopping

c. Come to a complete stop, flash high beams, and complete the turn

d. Make the turn without stopping if the way is clear

30. What does a yellow diamond-shaped sign with a black arrow pointed at an angle mean?

a. Sharp turn ahead

b. No passing zone

c. Divided highway ahead

d. Warning of a school zone

31. If a vehicle abruptly cuts in front of you, creating a potential hazard, your first action should be to:

a. Take your foot off the gas pedal

b. Honk and flash your headlights

c. Quickly switch lanes

d. Speed up to create more distance

32. The suggested placement of hands on the wheel is:

a. One hand on the wheel and the other at the passenger backrest.

b. Both hands together at the top center of the wheel.

c. Both hands equally apart in the 9 and 3 or 8 and 4 clock positions.

d. One hand in the 12 o'clock position, the other in the 6 o'clock position.

33. If a pedestrian begins crossing after the "Don't Walk" signal starts flashing and is still in the crosswalk when your light turns green, you should:

a. Proceed carefully around the pedestrian
b. Flash your lights to signal them to hurry
c. Honk to alert the pedestrian to walk faster
d. Wait until the pedestrian has fully crossed before moving forward

34. When there are two lanes that turn together, drivers must:

a. Make eye contact with the other drivers through the turn
b. Begin and end in the lane they started their turn from.
c. Both A and B
d. None of the above

35. Emergency hazard lights are to be used:

a. In heavy rain, snow, or fog when visibility is significantly reduced
b. If your car breaks down on a roadway
c. Both A and B
d. When making more than one lane change

36. When approaching an intersection with a solid green traffic light, the proper action is:

a. Stop and wait for the light to turn red
b. Slow down and proceed with caution
c. Proceed through the intersection if it is safe to do so
d. Slow down and yield the right-of-way to all other vehicles

37. Which of these is true regarding minors in cars?

a. It is lawful to leave a child under 6 years old if supervised by a 9 year old
b. It is lawful to leave a child under 6 unattended for 15 minutes
c. It is lawful to leave a child under 6 unattended as long as they have a cell phone
d. It is unlawful to leave a child under 6 unattended

38. It is important to take breaks when traveling long distances because

a. It is dangerous to drive when fatigued
b. Driving continuously for long blocks of time will affect the driver's focus
c. Both A and B
d. None of the above

39. If there is no crosswalk and a pedestrian is crossing in your lane, you are to:

a. Stop and allow the pedestrian to cross safely
b. Honk to alert the pedestrian to hurry
c. Continue driving carefully around them
d. Speed up to pass before they reach your lane

40. What is the purpose of a crosswalk with white lines painted across the road?

a. To indicate the end of a no-parking zone
b. To mark lanes for bicycles
c. To indicate where pedestrians may cross the road
d. To create additional lanes for vehicles

41. When should turn signals be used while driving?

   a. Only when making a U-turn
   b. Only when merging onto a freeway
   c. Before changing lanes, turning, or merging
   d. Only when turning onto a one-way street

42. You are driving on a multilane road, and you see a vehicle with flashing blue or red lights behind you. What should you do?

   a. Speed up to get out of its way
   b. Move to the right and allow it to pass
   c. Stop in the lane you are in
   d. Slow down and maintain your speed

43. What is the minimum age to obtain a regular, non-probationary driver's license in California?

   a. 16 years old
   b. 17 years old
   c. 18 years old
   d. 21 years old

44. You are driving on a two-way road and wish to turn left at an intersection with a green light. What should you do?

   a. Proceed into the intersection and wait for a sufficient gap or for oncoming traffic to stop
   b. Wait behind the stop line until it's safe to turn left
   c. Turn left immediately since you have the right-of-way
   d. Sound your horn to signal your intent to turn left

45. What is a best practice to avoid collisions?

a. Always taking your right of way
b. Communicate with other drivers
c. Driving 5 miles below the speed limit at all times
d. None of the above

46. What is the minimum age to apply for a Commercial Class A or B driver's license in California?

a. 16 years old
b. 17 years old
c. 18 years old
d. 21 years old

47. What is the purpose of a white diamond-shaped sign with a black arrow?

a. Indicates a school zone
b. Shows the direction of a nearby hospital
c. Warns of a pedestrian crossing
d. Provides guidance for a specific lane or exit

48. You should drive using your low-beam headlights

a. In clear weather during the day
b. In heavy fog, rain, or snow
c. At all times to save energy
d. When approaching a green traffic light

49. What do two capital R letters on the road mean?

a. No right turn allowed on a red light
b. Right Road
c. Rough Ride

d. Railroad Crossing

50. What is the common cause of a locked wheel skid?

a. Braking too hard
b. Accelerating too quickly
c. Turning too sharply
d. Braking too early

Answers
1. c 2. c 3. d 4. b 5. d 6. c 7. b 8. d 9. d 10. a
11. c 12. d 13. b 14. b 15. a 16. a 17. a 18. a 19. d 20. c
21. c 22. c 23. b 24. b 25. b 26. c 27. a 28. c 29. a 30. a
31. a 32. c 33. d 34. b 35. c 36. c 37. d 38. c 39. a 40. c
41. c 42. b 43. c 44. a 45. b 46. c 47. d 48. b 49. d 50. a

PRACTICE EXAM 1

It's time to put your knowledge to the test with these practice exams. Remember, this mirrors what you might face on the actual DMV test. Let's get started!

INSTRUCTIONS:

- Ensure you are in a quiet space where you won't be disturbed.
- Have a pencil or pen and a piece of paper handy to jot down your answers.
- Read each question carefully. Consider every detail as it might lead you to the correct answer.
- Do not rush. Though the actual DMV exam is timed, this practice test isn't. Take your time to understand each question and think over your answer.
- Once you've tackled all questions, proceed to the Answer Key to check how you've done.
- Review any questions you got wrong and make sure you understand the correct answer to avoid repeating the same mistake in the future.

PRACTICE EXAM

1. As you approach an intersection, the light goes from green to yellow; you should

    a. Speed up to clear the intersection
    b. Stop if it is still safe to do so, or go through if stopping would be unsafe
    c. Turn on hazard lights
    d. Flash high beams and honk horn to alert other drivers you're approaching

2. A red and white sign with a triangular shape means

    a. Yield the right-of-way
    b. Stop ahead
    c. No right on red
    d. Railroad crossing ahead

3. Drivers are to _____ prior to proceeding if behind a school bus that has flashing red lights and an extended stop sign.

    a. Lower their window and yell their intentions
    b. Stop and wait for the lights to stop flashing and for the stop sign to be retracted
    c. Flash their high beams and honk their horn
    d. Stop, wait 3 seconds, and look both ways

4. A yield sign means as you approach, you must

    a. Flash your high beams
    b. Reduce your speed and be prepared to give the right of way to other traffic
    c. Merge into traffic without stopping

d. Speed up to merge quickly

5. When parking on a downhill slope, you should turn your wheels

    a. Toward the curb
    b. Away from the curb
    c. Parallel to the curb
    d. It doesn't matter

6. If you are involved in a collision, you must exchange information with the other party. What information should you provide?

    a. Your name, driver's license, proof of insurance, and vehicle registration.
    b. Your name and insurance information only.
    c. Your driver's license number and phone number.
    d. Your name and nothing else.

7. To avoid glare from the headlights of an approaching vehicle, you should

    a. Look to the right side of the road
    b. Look to the left side of the road
    c. Look straight ahead
    d. Turn on your high beams

8. _____ is the minimum following distance you should maintain behind the vehicle ahead of you:

    a. 3 seconds
    b. 4 seconds
    c. 10 seconds
    d. 15 seconds

9. What is a best practice if you are on the right lane and see traffic merging into your lane?

   a. Speed up to discourage them from getting in front of you
   b. Try to create space for the merging traffic
   c. Come to a stop to let them in
   d. Ignore them since it is your right of way

10. When driving on the freeway behind a large truck, how should you position your vehicle?

   a. Close behind the truck to reduce wind resistance
   b. At the same distance as you would follow a car
   c. In the truck's blind spot to avoid wind gusts
   d. Farther behind the truck than if you were following a passenger vehicle

11. Drivers shall not exceed _____ in residential areas unless a sign indicates a different speed:

   a. 15 mph
   b. 25 mph
   c. 35 mph
   d. 20 mph

12. When parallel parking, you should be within _____ from the curb:

   a. 1 foot
   b. 18 inches
   c. 2 feet
   d. 3 feet

13. What is the minimum age to apply for a regular Class C driver's license in California?

a. 16 years old
b. 17 years old
c. 18 years old
d. 21 years old

14. What should you do if, as you approach a railroad crossing, it starts flashing red lights and its gates are lowered?

a. Stop and wait until the lights stop flashing and the gates are raised
b. If you think you can make it speed up, the train must yield to you
c. Cross the tracks if no train is visible
d. Honk your horn and proceed

15. If the vehicle begins to skid:

a. The wheel should be turned in the direction of the skid
b. Press very hard on your brake pedal
c. Turn the steering wheel back and forth quickly and brake forcefully
d. Accelerate to gain control

16. What is the maximum BAC limit for drivers 21 and older?

a. 0.08%
b. 0.01%
c. 0.10%
d. Any level as long as the person is coherent

17. When driving in foggy conditions, you should use your

    a. High beams
    b. Low beams
    c. Parking lights
    d. Hazard lights

18. _____ to indicate a left turn.

    a. Extend your left arm and hand upward
    b. Extend your left arm and hand horizontally
    c. Extend your right arm and hand upward
    d. Extend your right arm and hand horizontally

19. When can you use a cell phone while driving without a hands-free device?

    a. Whenever you are late for work or school and can prove your commitment time
    b. Only when making a call
    c. Only when sending a text message
    d. In case of emergencies

20. If your vehicle's brakes fail while driving, you should

    a. Pump the brakes to build up brake fluid pressure
    b. Shift to a lower gear
    c. Gradually use the parking brake
    d. All of the above

21. What position should your front wheels be in if you park uphill next to a curb?

    a. Turned away from the curb
    b. Turned toward the curb

c. Straight and parallel to the curb

d. Turned left

22. What should you do If you encounter a pedestrian at a cross-walk using a white cane or guide dog?

a. Honk your horn to alert them to your presence

b. Slow down and proceed with caution

c. Stop and wait for them to cross the street

d. Drive around them quickly

23. What is the penalty for a first-time conviction of driving under the influence (DUI)?

a. A fine up to $1000

b. Up to 6 months in jail

c. Vehicle will be impounded

d. All of the above

24. Drivers are to signal their intention to turn at least _____ feet before making the turn.

a. 400 feet

b. 350 feet

c. 50 feet

d. 100 feet

25. When making a lane change from a slower speed lane to a faster one, you should:

a. Assure the gap between cars is large enough and begin accelerating while performing the lane change

b. Assure the gap between cars is large enough and maintain your current speed while performing the lane change

c. Assure the gap between cars is large enough and slow down while performing the lane change

d. None of the above

26. Why is additional space in front of a large truck necessary?

a. To allow other vehicles to merge

b. To improve fuel efficiency for the truck

c. For smaller vehicles to pass safely

d. So the truck driver has enough room to stop safely

27. If you are approaching a railroad crossing with no warning signals or gates, you should

a. Speed up to cross the tracks quickly

b. Reduce speed and prepare to stop if necessary

c. Continue at the same speed

d. Change lanes to avoid the tracks

28. In the event a driver fails to stop for a school bus with flashing red lights and an extended stop sign, the repercussion is.

a. A warning

b. A small fine

c. A large fine and a possible suspension of your driver's license

d. Community service

29. Drivers shall not exceed _____ at an uncontrolled (blin intersection.

a. 40 mph

b. 45 mph

c. 15 mph

d. 10 mph

30. When turning on slick roads, you should:

a. Reduce your speed more than usual
b. Maintain your usual speed
c. Increase your speed slightly
d. Make the turn as sharp as possible

31. When are drivers permitted to drive through "safety zones"?

a. During rush hour
b. Under no circumstances
c. When no pedestrians are present
d. between 30 minutes after sunrise and 30 minutes before sunset

32. When approaching a curve or hill where you can't see ahead, you should

a. Increase your speed to get through it more quickly
b. Keep your speed constant and stay in your lane
c. Reduce speed on approach and be prepared to stop if necessary
d. Switch lanes to pass slower vehicles

33. What is a possible consequence for the illegal use of a disabled placard?

a. Community service
b. A warning from authorities
c. Revocation of the placard, a fine, and/or jail time
d. Only a fine

34. When driving on a two-lane road, you should

    a. Drive on the right side of your lane
    b. Drive in the center of your lane
    c. Drive on the left side of your lane
    d. Alternate between the right and left sides of your lane

35. When behind a vehicle, where should a motorcyclist be positioned?

    a. 10 seconds behind the vehicle
    b. As close to the blind spot of the vehicle as possible, the noise of the motorcycle will alert the driver the motorcyclist is there
    c. In a place where the driver of the vehicle can see the motorcyclist with the rearview mirror
    d. Anywhere; the driver of the vehicle is responsible for looking for the motorcyclist

36. It is _____ to do a lane change while going through an intersection.

    a. Safe
    b. Illegal
    c. Legal while the sun is out
    d. None of the above

37. Which of the following is true about pedestrian crosswalks?

    a. The right-of-way must always be given to pedestrians at crosswalks
    b. Pedestrians must yield to vehicles at crosswalks
    c. Vehicles must stop only if pedestrians are in the same lane as the vehicle
    d. Vehicles must stop only if pedestrians are in marked crosswalks

38. When using your high beams, you should switch to low beams at _____ of an approaching vehicle.

a. 1000 feet
b. 500 feet
c. 1500 feet
d. None are correct

39. When you see a solid yellow line on your side of the road, it means

a. You may pass if the way is clear
b. You may pass with caution
c. You may not pass
d. You may pass if you are in a hurry

40. In regard to driving in California, the "basic speed law" is best described as

a. It's basic knowledge that the fast lane on the freeway is to speed
b. Drivers are expected to drive at a reasonable and prudent speed for current conditions
c. It is basic knowledge that the slow lane is to drive significantly below the posted speed limit
d. You may drive above the posted speed limit if you are passing another vehicle

41. Which of the following is true about a flashing red traffic light?

a. Treat it like a stop sign
b. Slow down and proceed with caution
c. Speed up and proceed through the intersection
d. It has no special meaning

42. When driving on a one-way street with three or more lanes of traffic, to pass, you should use

a. The left lanes
b. The center lane
c. Any available lane
d. The far right lane

43. You should use your horn when

a. You are frustrated with other drivers
b. You are approaching a blind intersection
c. You must alert another driver or pedestrian of an impending collision
d. You want to make a vehicle move faster

44. To safely pass a bicyclist on the road, you should

a. Honk your horn loudly to warn them
b. Pass them quickly with a close clearance
c. Leave at least three feet of clearance as you pass them
d. Pass them only if they signal you to do so

45. When you see solid white lines on the lanes, it means

a. You are approaching a construction zone
b. You are on a one-way street
c. You should merge to the left
d. You should stay within the lane and not change lanes

46. You are approaching a turn with a yellow warning sign of 25 mph, and it is raining; you should

a. Pull over and wait for the rain to stop to complete the turn
b. Turn at whatever the official speed limit is for the road

c. Reduce your speed to 15 to 20 miles per hour for the turn

d. Maintain a speed of at least 30 miles per hour to compensate for the lost traction

47. Which of the following is true about driving in heavy rain?

a. Use your high beams to improve visibility

b. Increase your speed to get through it more quickly

c. Reduce your speed, turn on your headlights, and increase following distance

d. Follow closely behind the vehicle in front of you

48. If you drive on a surface that is slippery, such as snow or ice, you should:

a. Use a larger-than-normal following distance and drive as slowly as needed to maintain control of the vehicle

b. Drive at the posted speed limit and brake as late as possible for less slipping

c. Use your cruise control to maintain speed

d. Make sudden turns to maintain better control

49. If you are involved in a collision and your vehicle is blocking traffic, you should:

a. Keep windows raised, doors locked and avoid interacting with anyone until emergency personnel arrive

b. Move your vehicle off the road, if possible

c. Exit the vehicle and open all doors including the trunk to have the car be as big as possible

d. Turn the vehicle sideways so it's easier for approaching drivers to see

50. In California, drivers _____ as a consequence for driving without auto insurance:

a. Receive a warning
b. Get a small fine
c. Have their Driver's license suspended
d. None of the above

PRACTICE EXAM 2

1. With a class C license, a person may drive

   a. A three-axle vehicle weighing less than 6,000 pounds
   b. A motorcycle
   c. A commercial bus
   d. All of the above

2. To pass a bicyclist in a narrow lane while a vehicle is coming from the opposite direction, it's best to:

   a. Speed up to pass the bicyclist quickly
   b. Move closer to the bicyclist to create more space for the oncoming vehicle
   c. Slow down and wait for the oncoming vehicle to pass before overtaking the bicyclist
   d. Honk to alert the bicyclist to move over

3. Sharrows on the road

   a. Indicate the presence of a bicycle lane
   b. Are regulatory signs reminding drivers to share the road with bicyclists
   c. Mark pedestrian crosswalks
   d. None of the above

4. You are legally required to _____ when an emergency vehicle, using a siren and red lights, approaches you.

   a. Honk your horn
   b. Pull over and stop
   c. Increase your speed
   d. Proceed as usual

5. Alcohol and tobacco are _____

   a. Moderate Potency drugs
   b. Hallucinogenic drugs
   c. Gateway drugs
   d. Prescription drugs

6. When being passed by another vehicle, you should

   a. Slow down and let them pass
   b. Maintain your speed
   c. Speed up to avoid being passed
   d. Change lanes immediately

7. A green arrow on a traffic signal means?

   a. Stop
   b. Yield to oncoming traffic
   c. Proceed in the direction of the arrow if it's safe to do so
   d. Prepare to make a U-turn

8. Looking both ways approaching intersections is an example of

   a. Conversion
   b. Velocitation
   c. Scanning
   d. Synergy

9. Most minor traffic violations come off your driving record after

   a. 12 months
   b. 18 months
   c. 24 months
   d. 36 months

10. These types of vehicles, due to their size, appear to be moving slower than they actually are.

   a. Mopeds
   b. Golf Carts
   c. Trains
   d. Sport Utility Vehicles

11. When attempting a right turn with a red light, you need to make sure that:

   a. There are no Pedestrians in the crosswalk
   b. There is nobody doing a U-Turn
   c. There is no sign prohibiting a right turn with a red light
   d. All of the above

12. What is the name of the point system used by the DMV to track traffic violations?

   a. N.O.T.S. (Negligent Operator Treatment System)
   b. N.O.C.R. (Not On California Roads)
   c. N.O.O.R. (Not On Our Roads)
   d. N.D.O.S. (New Driver Operation Score)

13. When is it illegal to smoke in a car?

   a. When driving over the speed limit
   b. When the windows are rolled up

c. When there is a pet in the vehicle

d. When a person under 18 years of age is in the car

14. Depressants

a. Cause the central nervous system to speed up

b. Slow down the central nervous system

c. Do not have any effect on the central nervous system

d. Cause hallucinations

15. When are you required to provide proof of insurance to law enforcement?

a. Only during a traffic stop

b. At a vehicle registration renewal

c. Only if requested by other drivers

d. When involved in an accident or stopped by an officer

16. When stopping at a railroad crossing with multiple tracks, you should:

a. Cross immediately after the first train passes

b. Stop halfway across the tracks to check for other trains

c. Wait only if you see another train approaching

d. Wait to proceed until you have a clear view of all tracks

17. An underage driver may lose his or her license with this amount of alcohol in the body:

a. 0.02%

b. 0.05%

c. 0.08%

d. Any amount since they have "zero tolerance"

18. The force of impact can be reduced by allowing objects to come to a stop over

    a. Short distances
    b. Medium distances
    c. Greater distances
    d. None of the above

19. Of the following, which increase stopping distances and increase the severity of collisions.

    a. Adjusting the radio
    b. Driving downhill
    c. Driving at high speeds
    d. Night time driving

20. If you encounter an animal on the road, the best action is to

    a. Accelerate to scare it away
    b. Turn sharply to avoid it
    c. Wait for it to clear the road on its own
    d. Honk your horn to scare it away

21. Pedestrians should

    a. Follow traffic laws
    b. Wear reflective clothing when it's dark out
    c. Both a and b
    d. None of the above

22. Most drivers believe they are _____ than other drivers

    a. More skillful and safer
    b. Less experienced

c. More reckless

d. None of the above

23. If you have reason to believe you are sharing the road with an impaired driver, it's safest to be

a. Behind the suspected impaired driver

b. In front of the suspected impaired driver

c. In a lane to the side of the suspected impaired driver

d. None of the above

24. If an object's speed doubles, what is the effect on the object's kinetic energy?

a. No change

b. It is increased twofold

c. Is quadrupled

d. Depends on its mass

25. An example of a divided highway is when it is separated by

a. A central divider

b. A solid concrete barrier or metallic guardrail

c. Two pairs of double yellow lines at two or more feet apart

d. All of the above

26. Of the following, which is true regarding driving in another driver's blind spot.

a. Honk your horn to alert the driver you are in their blind spot

b. Do your best to stay steady in the blind spot

c. Change lanes immediately

d. It's best to reposition to be slightly ahead or behind to allow for the other driver to see you

27. **For drivers turning left, what is the meaning of a flashing yellow arrow?**

a. Wait for it to flash green to turn
b. Wait for it to turn into a solid yellow arrow to turn
c. It alerts of an oncoming emergency vehicle
d. The left turn is allowed after yielding to pedestrians and oncoming traffic

28. _____ **is the minimum age to obtain a learner's permit.**

a. 14 1/2
b. 16 ½
c. 15 1/2
d. 17 1/2

29. **Children shall ride in an approved passenger restraint system or a booster seat unless they are:**

a. 6 years of age and more than 55 lbs
b. 7 years of age or older and more than 65 lbs
c. at least 8 year of age or a minimum height of 4'9"
d. None of the above

30. **If you approach a vehicle from the rear with your high beams on, at what distance do you need to switch them to your regular beams?**

a. 1000 feet
b. 300 feet
c. 100 feet
d. ¾ mile

31. A solid yellow light at an intersection means

    a. Come to a stop, unless you are already within the intersection
    b. Maintenance is being done
    c. It will turn into a flashing yellow soon
    d. Accelerate to enter legally

32. When waiting inside an intersection to turn left, you should:

    a. Signal and turn your wheels slightly left
    b. Signal and turn your wheels slightly right
    c. Signal and keep your wheels straight
    d. Wait until the light turns red to turn

33. It is legal to drive on the emergency shoulder if

    a. It is never legal; it is for emergency use only
    b. You are late for work and have an official Government job
    c. You honk your horn to be responsible and alert other drivers
    d. You make hand gestures, and the other drivers acknowledge you

34. Following the flow of traffic means

    a. Drive as fast as everyone else, no matter if it is above the speed limit, or you will be cited for going too slow
    b. Take your foot off the accelerator when going downhill and cruise to save fuel
    c. You should pass anyone doing less than the speed limit
    d. Within reason, drive at approximately the same speed as everyone else

35. Common causes of car crashes include

a. Exceeding the speed limit
b. Making an improper turn
c. Violating the right-of-way rules
d. All of the above

36. What does BAC stand for?

a. Blood Alcohol Control
b. Blood Alcohol Count
c. Blood Alcohol Casualty
d. Blood Alcohol Content

37. What will happen if you pass a school bus that is stopped with its red lights flashing?

a. Receive a warning
b. Be fined up to $1,000
c. Be required to attend traffic school
d. Be fined up to $500

38. Which is true in regard to motorcycles lane usage allowance?

a. They are allowed ½ of the lane
b. They are allowed the full width of the lane
c. They are required to split lanes and not take a full width
d. Both A and C

39. All vehicle rear stop lights must be _____:

a. White
b. Orange
c. Red
d. Brown

40. All vehicle stop lights shall be visible at a minimum distance of _____:

   a. ½ mile
   b. 500 feet
   c. 1000 feet
   d. ¾ mile

41. A curb painted green means

   a. Parking for a limited time, a sign usually displays the time allowed
   b. Parking for an unlimited time
   c. Parking for compact vehicles only
   d. All of the above

42. A curb painted yellow means

   a. Parking for passenger vehicles only
   b. Parking for freight unloading; the driver must remain with the vehicle
   c. Parking for emergency vehicles
   d. All of the above

43. A blue-painted curb signifies parking allowed

   a. For residents only
   b. For handicapped parking only
   c. For commercial vehicles only
   d. For motorcycles only

44. Driving off the road to pass another vehicle is permitted:

   a. Anytime it's safe
   b. In rural areas

c. Never

d. When the other driver signals you to pass

45. After a change of address, the Department of Motor Vehicles shall be notified within _____.

a. 12 days

b. 72 hours

c. 10 days

d. 48 hours

46. If you sold your vehicle, you must notify the Department of Motor Vehicles within _____.

a. 30 days

b. 5 days

c. 72 hours

d. None are correct

47. Regarding a bike lane prior to making a right turn, you should

a. Assure not to touch the bike lane

b. Speed up to enter the bike lane ahead of any bicyclist since vehicles go faster

c. Both A and B

d. Enter the bicycle lane the last 200 feet

48. Parents need to be alert to the following dangers involving cars and infants:

a. Forgetting an infant in a hot car

b. Having an infant follow them to the car and injuring or killing them by not seeing them as they begin to drive

c. Both a and b

d. None of the above

49. For maximum safety, how far ahead should you scan?

    a. Minimum 5 to 8 seconds
    b. Minimum 7 to 10seconds
    c. Minimum 10 to 15seconds
    d. Minimum 25 seconds

50. A yellow center line, which is broken, signifies what?

    a. Passing is allowed if safe
    b. No passing allowed
    c. The road is under construction
    d. A pedestrian crosswalk

Practice Exam 2: Answer Sheet
1. a) 2. c) 3. b) 4. b) 5. c) 6. b) 7. c) 8. c) 9. d) 10. c)
11. d) 12. a) 13. d) 14. b) 15. d) 16. d) 17. d) 18. c) 19. c) 20. c)
21. c) 22. a) 23. a) 24. c) 25. d) 26. d) 27. d) 28. c) 29. c) 30. b)
31. a) 32. c) 33. a) 34. d) 35. d) 36. d) 37. b) 38. b) 39. c) 40. b)
41. a) 42. b) 43. b) 44. c) 45. c) 46. b) 47. d) 48. c) 49. c) 50. a)

PRACTICE EXAM 3

1. What does an orange sign with black lettering indicate?

   a. A school zone
   b. Construction zone
   c. A hospital zone
   d. A scenic route

2. Unless the speed limit would be exceeded, driving at a speed below the flow of traffic:

   a. Interferes with traffic and you could be cited
   b. Improves fuel efficiency
   c. Improves overall safety
   d. None of the above

3. Drivers are required to file an SR1 report with the DMV if there is a collision, and

   a. The collision results in injury
   b. The collision results in property damage in excess of $1,000
   c. Both a and b
   d. None of the above

4. The hand gesture to indicate "stop" is:

a. Extend your left hand out the driver's side window and move it up and down
b. Point your left hand downward out the driver's side window
c. Extend your left hand straight out the driver's side window
d. Waive your left hand in a circular motion outside the driver's side window

5. You should allow a larger space cushion than usual when stopping:

a. Uphill
b. At dusk or dawn
c. Downhill
d. On long flat roads

6. You may legally make a right turn with an arrow that is red

a. After slowing down to verify if it is safe to proceed
b. Never; you must wait for a green light or for the red arrow to disappear
c. Once it turns into a flashing red arrow
d. Only during daylight so other drivers and pedestrians see you better

7. When is it legal to block an intersection?

a. During rush hour traffic
b. When there is a sign indicating it's allowed
c. Never
d. Only if you have a valid reason

8. Commercial vehicles have

a. Fewer blind spots than regular passenger vehicles
b. A greater number of blind spots than passenger vehicles
c. The same number of blind spots as passenger vehicles
d. No blind spots

9. What is the meaning of the "end school zone" sign?

a. School buses are not allowed to pull over past this zone
b. Parents are no longer allowed to pick up children
c. Children no longer get the right of way
d. The end of the 25 mile per hour school zone

10. What is the minimum liability insurance amount acceptable in California?

a. $7,500
b. $12,500
c. $15,000
d. $20,000

11. What is the definition of California's Move Over Law?

a. Drivers must slow down and move to the left when approaching an intersection
b. Drivers must move over and stop for all emergency vehicles with flashing lights, regardless of the situation
c. Drivers are required to change lanes in all construction zones
d. Drivers must slow down or move over a lane when approaching stationary emergency vehicles, tow trucks, or utility vehicles displaying flashing lights

12. Left turns from multilane one-way streets onto a one-way street should be started from what lane?

  a. The farthest left
  b. Any middle lane
  c. The farthest right
  d. Any lane

13. If you get a green light but notice the intersection is not clear of traffic, you should

  a. Proceed quickly to avoid holding up traffic
  b. Stay out of the intersection until it clears
  c. Honk your horn to alert other drivers
  d. Flash your headlights to signal the right-of-way

14. If you intend to pass another vehicle, you should:

  a. Expect the other driver to slow down
  b. Assume the other driver will create space for you to return to your lane
  c. Signal and immediately move into the passing lane without hesitation
  d. Not rely on the other driver to make room for you to merge back into your lane

15. When is it legal to stop on the shoulder of the freeway?

  a. To change a flat tire
  b. If the engine is over heating
  c. In case of an emergency
  d. All of the above

16. Which of these will cause you to be charged with a DUI:

a. You use over-the-counter medication that prohibits driving
b. You exhibit signs of being impaired and marijuana is found in your system
c. You drive after using prescribed medication, which prohibits driving
d. All of the above

17. You approach an intersection with a red light, and there is a police officer who is in the intersection and waves you to proceed. What should you do?

a. Follow the police officer's instructions and go through even though the light is red
b. Stop and point out to the police officer the danger of waving you through with a red light
c. Stop and wait for the light to turn green
d. Speed up to show you clearly are following the officer's instructions

18. If you hit or kill an animal, you should

a. Administer CPR
b. Approach it and move it to evaluate how badly injured the animal is
c. Stop and call animal services, the local Police, or CHP
d. Place the animal in your car and rush to a hospital

19. A passenger having an open alcoholic container:

a. Is lawful
b. Is unlawful
c. Is lawful if the passenger is 21 or older
d. Is lawful if the passenger is sleeping

20. During winter months, which of these should be removed from you windows prior to driving?

    a. Ice
    b. Snow
    c. Frost
    d. All of the above

21. When two sets of double yellow lines are present:

    a. Passing is allowed if safe
    b. You are approaching a merge of lanes
    c. They are not to be crossed for any reason
    d. You're allowed to cross them if driving a high-occupancy vehicle

22. You are driving on a section of the freeway where the maximum speed limit is 65 and the flow of traffic is 70. You may legally drive

    a. At the flow of traffic (70)
    b. No faster than 65, as that is the maximum speed limit posted
    c. Up to 75, but only in the left lane
    d. 80, as long as you keep up with the fastest vehicle

23. If you get tired after driving for a long period of time, the best thing to do is

    a. Have an energy drink
    b. Turn on the car's air conditioning
    c. Go faster to get your destination before your tiredness gets worse
    d. Pull over and get some rest

24. Which of these is a danger to watch out for when driving in neighborhoods:

a. Children that could rush into the street
b. Drivers backing up into the street from their driveways
c. Both a and b are correct
d. None of the above

25. Increase the following distance when:

a. There is adverse weather
b. Following large trucks
c. Following a motorcycle
d. All of the above

26. When are you legally allowed to drive with only your parking lights on?

a. During heavy fog
b. During a power outage
c. Never
d. When driving in a parking lot

27. When two yellow lines are in the center median and _____, then you may legally pass.

a. You clearly see no oncoming traffic
b. The closest line to you is broken
c. The inside lines are dashed
d. You are driving a motorcycle

28. Scanning means:

a. Continually moving your eyes looking for potential hazards
b. Staring at the road ahead without moving your eyes

c. Accelerating quickly and slowing down hard to discourage anyone from being near you

d. Using your smartphone while driving

29. When approaching intersections, drivers should

a. Focus only on the traffic signal
b. Look both ways prior to entering
c. Speed up to get through quickly
d. Depend on the traffic behind them to warn of hazards

30. A commercial semi-truck ahead of you has signaled that it will turn right. The truck may have to

a. Make a left turn instead
b. Swing left first to generate enough space to complete the right turn
c. Stop in the middle of the intersection
d. Turn right without any issues

31. If you are in a nervous, scared or highly emotional state of mind:

a. Take time to gather your emotions prior to driving
b. Take a drive as soon as possible to help you clear your mind
c. Ensure you have other distractions while you drive to keep your emotions in check
d. Both B and C

32. If your turn signal stops working, you must use hand signals: _____ to indicate a right turn.

a. Stick your right hand out of the window and point straight up
b. Point the left hand straight up out the driver's side.
c. Wave your hand in a circle

d. Stick the right hand out the window and point straight down

33. If the vehicle breaks down, it is best for you to

a. Get off the road and get to the shoulder
b. Turn on the hazard lights
c. Both a and b
d. None of the above

34. _____ are required to stop prior to crossing railroad tracks.

a. Bicycles and motorcycles
b. Passenger cars
c. Buses and commercial vehicles carrying hazardous materials
d. Electric vehicles

35. When you tailgate other drivers

a. You increase your chances of a collision by reducing your safety buffer
b. You encourage them to speed up
c. You make it easier to communicate with hand signals
d. You become a courteous driver

36. You have waited on a red light, and it turns green; a good habit is to

a. Look both ways before proceeding to ensure nobody is running the light
b. Immediately accelerate as quickly as possible so as not to anger the drivers behind you
c. Remain stopped for at least 5 seconds to ensure the intersection is truly safe

d. Move in and stop in the middle of the intersection and look both ways

37. When should you check your rearview mirrors?

a. Only when changing lanes
b. Only when stopping at an intersection
c. Before making a turn
d. Often, to see how traffic is moving behind you

38. The elements required to stop are

a. Reaction, perception, and stopping distance
b. Inertia, gravity, and wind speed
c. Time of day, weight of vehicle, and type of road
d. All of the above

39. When driving behind large semi-trucks

a. Stay very close to reduce wind resistance
b. Keep a following distance of greater than three seconds as your view of what is happening in front of the semi-truck is obstructed.
c. Overtake them quickly to avoid their blind spots
d. Use their slipstream to save fuel

40. Flashing yellow lights at intersections mean

a. Proceed with caution, but no need to slow down
b. Slow down and proceed with caution
c. Speed up to get through the intersection before the lights change
d. Stop immediately and wait for further instructions

41. It is illegal to park within _____ of a fire hydrant

a. 3 feet
b. 12 feet
c. 15 feet
d. 30 feet

42. It is lawful to drive to the left side of two solid yellow lines if:

a. You check, and there is no oncoming traffic
b. Your destination is close and on the left side of the road
c. Never
d. No sign prohibits it

43. As you approach a turn to prevent skidding, what should you do?

a. Speed up before the turn
b. Reduce your speed prior to the turn
c. Maintain your current speed
d. Slam on the brakes during the turn

44. What should you do if you see a train as you approach an uncontrolled railroad crossing?

a. Stop before the crossing and wait for the train to finish going through
b. Stop on the tracks
c. Stop, exit the vehicle, and waive at the train conductor to establish your right-of-way
d. Speed up to beat the train

45. When a transit vehicle signals its intent to merge back onto the main road, what action should you take?

a. Maintain your speed and position
b. Speed up
c. Yield
d. None of the above

46. What must drivers do when it rains?

a. Turn off their headlights
b. Use windshield wipers and turn on headlights
c. Drive faster to get out of the rain
d. Use the hazard lights instead of headlights

47. A center turn lane can be used for how many feet to complete a left turn?

a. 50 feet
b. 100 feet
c. 200 feet
d. 300 feet

48. Left turns on red lights are permitted _____:

a. Whenever the other drivers signal for you to go
b. Only if no other vehicles are present
c. When turning from a one-way street onto another one-way street
d. Only during nighttime hours

49. What is considered a proper stop at an intersection?

a. Slow down and if no danger, proceed with caution
b. Stop fully and count to three

c. Stop the vehicle fully, then look left, right and left again
d. Slow down almost to a stop, if not a multi lane road, proceed without stopping

50. It is unlawful to follow an emergency vehicle closer than

a. 50 feet
b. 100 feet
c. 200 feet
d. 300 feet

Practice Exam 3: Answer Sheet
1. b) 2. a) 3. c) 4. b) 5. c) 6. b) 7. c) 8. b) 9 d) 10. c)
11. d) 12. a) 13. b) 14. d) 15. d) 16. d) 17. a) 18. c) 19. b) 20. d)
21. c) 22. b) 23. d) 24. c) 25. d) 26. c) 27. b) 28. a) 29. b) 30. b)
31. a) 32. b) 33. c) 34. c) 35. a) 36. a) 37. d) 38. a) 39. b) 40. b)
41. c) 42. c) 43. b) 44. a) 45. c) 46. b) 47. c) 48. c) 49. c) 50. d)

PRACTICE EXAM 4

1. Roads are most likely to freeze quickly when they are:

  a. Covered by salt
  b. Wet
  c. Shaded
  d. Isolated

2. Why is it important for motorcyclists to develop good visual search patterns?

  a. To avoid speeding
  b. To blend in with other vehicles
  c. Because motorists have difficulty seeing motorcyclists
  d. To conserve fuel

3. Drivers are to stop when approaching a railroad crossing equipped with warning lights but no gates and _____:

  a. The road is wet
  b. You see a green light
  c. The warning lights are flashing red
  d. The train is in sight

4. Which of these traffic citations are assessed two points on the driving record?

    a. Street racing
    b. DUI
    c. Felony hit and run
    d. All of the above

5. The following will result in getting cited for Driving Under the Influence

    a. Consuming marijuana and driving
    b. Driving a motorized boat after consuming marijuana
    c. Riding a horse on a roadway and having a BAC of .09%
    d. All of the above

6. Which statement is true regarding bicycle riders?

    a. They have no rights or responsibilities
    b. They have the same rights and responsibilities as car drivers
    c. They have more rights than car drivers
    d. They have fewer rights than car drivers

7. _____ is a defensive driving technique:

    a. Road rage
    b. Tailgating
    c. Having an escape route
    d. Always driving 10 to 15 miles per hour slower than everyone else

8. What does HOV stand for?

    a. High oversize vehicle
    b. Hot operating vehicle

c. High occupancy vehicle

d. None of the above

9. What is the penalty for refusing to comply with a chemical test of your blood alcohol content when arrested for drunk driving?

a. A fine

b. Driving privilege suspended for at least twelve months

c. Required to attend traffic school

d. Receive a warning

10. When approaching intersections that have had a green light for a long time, drivers should

a. Speed up to enter before it turns yellow

b. Anticipate it could go to yellow and prepare to stop

c. Speed up but for safety reasons honk your horn within 200 feet to alert others you are committed to going through it

d. To be safe stop if it has been green more than 15 seconds as the yellow light is inevitably coming soon

11. If a person gets their Driver's License revoked, they can reapply:

a. after 6 months

b. After the period of revocation

c. After attending traffic school

d. After serving jail time

12. When making turns, it's best to _____ your speed:

a. Maintain

b. Increase

c. Ignore

d. Reduce

13. Traffic fines in construction zones are usually _____

    a. Cut in half
    b. Charged the same amount as any citation
    c. Charged at four times the amount
    d. Charged at twice the amount

14. What is the recommended course of action if you exit a freeway and encounter a downhill curved exit ramp?

    a. Speed up to merge quickly
    b. Slow to a safe speed before the curve
    c. Maintain the same speed
    d. Use your emergency brake

15. What does an ignition interlock device require the driver to do?

    a. Input the driving route of the driver so authorities always know their location.
    b. Take a breath test for alcohol each time the vehicle is started
    c. Have fingerprint taken before starting the vehicle
    d. Input the number of drinks taken into the device

16. If a person has consumed too much alcohol, among the choices provided, which one will speed up their body's alcohol metabolism and help them sober up in less time?

    a. Having at least 3 cups of coffee
    b. Having several energy drinks
    c. Taking a cold shower
    d. Only time can give the body the opportunity to process the alcohol

17. **This condition happens when driving long distances on monotonous roads:**

  a. Highway 101
  b. Route 66
  c. Highway hypnosis
  d. 4-wheel hallucination

18. **To whom should you give the right-of-way when waiting to make a left turn?**

  a. Cars coming from the opposite direction
  b. Oncoming vehicles turning right
  c. Pedestrians
  d. All of the above

19. **If you approach an area that has orange construction signs and traffic cones, you should**

  a. Speed up to get through the construction zone quickly
  b. Ignore the signs and continue as usual
  c. Be prepared for workers and slow-moving equipment
  d. Pull over to the side of the road

20. **Before crossing at an intersection without traffic signals or stop signs, pedestrians**

  a. Should get a running start
  b. Should make sure it is clear of traffic before attempting to cross
  c. Should force their way across even with traffic since they have the right of way
  d. All of the above

21. What is one of the most common causes of accidents?

    a. Proper signaling
    b. Wearing a seatbelt
    c. Improper turns
    d. Following speed limits

22. When there is a large amount of water on the road and it is deeply flooded, it is best to

    a. Speed up to cross the water as safely as possible
    b. Turn around, do not cross deep water
    c. Exit the vehicle and step in it to determine how deep it truly is
    d. Stop and wait to see what other drivers do

23. When should you use your high-beam headlights if it doesn't interfere with the vision of other drivers on the roadway?

    a. Only on foggy days
    b. Whenever you want
    c. Whenever you are having trouble seeing with your low-beam headlights
    d. Never use high beams

24. How should you check that your blind spot is free of any danger?

    a. Use your rearview mirror
    b. Use your side mirrors
    c. Look over your shoulder
    d. Honk your horn

25. In California, you can drive without wearing a seat belt if

a. Your car has front and side airbags
b. Your vehicle is equipped with collision assist
c. Your drive doesn't require you to enter the freeway
d. None of the above

26. In what situations may you use a center left turn lane?

a. Only for U-turns
b. To pass slower vehicles
c. To start or complete left turns
d. As a dedicated bicycle lane

27. What does smooth, gradual braking do for your driving?

a. Makes your vehicle go faster
b. Helps maintain tire pressure
c. Will lower your likelihood of being rear-ended
d. Saves fuel by 50% or more

28. What is true when you are in a turn lane controlled by an arrow and it turns green?

a. Proceed with no need to concern yourself with traffic
b. May proceed to turn in the direction of the arrow but must yield to traffic or pedestrians that are already in the intersection.
c. May proceed to turn and if needed weave between pedestrians
d. You can make any type of turn you want

29. Due to their size, _____ are at higher risk of not being seen if drivers don't carefully check their blind spots prior to lane changes.

a. Motorcyclists
b. Sport utility vehicles
c. Electric cars
d. Hybrid vehicles

30. What should you do when a vehicle in the lane to your right is stopped at a crosswalk?

a. Speed up to pass quickly
b. Honk your horn to signal them to move
c. Stop before you enter the crosswalk
d. Continue without stopping

31. When may you be considered a negligent driver based on your record's violation point count?

a. 4 points in 4 years
b. 4 points in 3 years
c. 4 points in 12 months
d. 3 points in 18 months

32. Bicyclists should

a. Obey traffic laws
b. Wear reflective clothing at night
c. Both a and b
d. None of the above

33. It is possible to lose your driving privileges due to

a. A conviction of reckless driving causing bodily injury to any person
b. DUI conviction
c. A conviction of speeding in a school zone
d. All of the above

34. For all right turns with multiple lanes, drivers must enter the _____ lane.

a. Leftmost lane
b. The middle lane when there are three lanes available
c. Rightmost lane
d. All of the above

35. Doing this improves your probability of surviving a collision:

a. Applying a lot of weight toward the door at the point of impact
b. Wearing seat belts
c. Jumping in the seat at the point of impact
d. Using a GPS

36. Drivers ought to stop prior to crossing railroad tracks if:

a. You are carrying 4 or more passengers
b. You don't trust that the control mechanisms are working
c. There is insufficient room for you to completely cross the tracks
d. You are driving a stick shift vehicle

37. What should your speed depend on?

a. The type of music you're listening to
b. Weather and road conditions
c. The time of day
d. The color of your car

38. What is an example of a 2-point violation?

a. Speeding
b. Running a red light
c. Reckless Driving
d. Parking in a no-parking zone

39. How many lane changes can you make at one time?

a. As many as safely possible
b. one
c. two during daylight
d. All of the above

40. What is the highest speed limit typically allowed on California Highways?

a. 30 mph
b. 45 mph
c. 60 mph
d. 65 mph

41. What occurs when your vehicle rides on top of the water on the road?

a. Hydroplaning
b. Skidding
c. Drifting

d. Floating

42. It is illegal to

a. Park on a yellow curb and remain in the vehicle while an occupant unloads cargo
b. Park 14 inches away from the curb
c. Park on the wrong side of the street
d. Switch lanes to pass a bicyclist

43. To reduce the possibility of a road rage incident, it is best to

a. Keep your cool
b. Avoid making eye contact
c. Not return angry gestures or engage in back-and-forth arguing
d. All of the above

44. Driving with underinflated tires

a. Gives you better gas mileage
b. Is dangerous and can cause loss of control if they blow out
c. Makes the tires last longer
d. both a and c

45. When followed by a tailgater, what is your course of action to remedy the unsafe situation?

a. Speed up to lose the tailgater
b. Brake suddenly to create distance
c. Signal and move to another lane as soon as it is safe
d. Roll down your window and wave

46. What should you do if your vehicle starts to hydroplane and you begin to skid?

a. Accelerate to regain control
b. Slam on the brakes
c. Take your foot off the accelerator so the vehicle slows down gradually
d. Steer sharply to the right

47. Which of these can cause you to hit a vehicle from behind?

a. Speeding
b. Following too closely
c. Texting and driving
d. All of the above

48. What is recommended if you go into an acceleration skid?

a. Slam on the brakes
b. Steer in the opposite direction
c. Ease off the gas pedal
d. Release the steering wheel and brace yourself for impact

49. To reduce the possibility of being involved in a road rage incident:

a. Drive aggressively to discourage the other driver from engaging with you.
b. Give an angry driver plenty of space
c. Honk your horn several times and flash your high beams
d. Maintain as much eye contact as possible with the angry driver

50. If a peace officer signals for you to pull over and you choose to ignore the officer and flee, what could be the consequence?

 a. A warning
 b. A small fine
 c. Jail time in the county jail for up to one year
 d. Community service and a written citation

Practice Exam 4: Answer Sheet
1. c) 2. c) 3. c) 4. d) 5. d) 6. b) 7. c) 8. c) 9. b) 10. b)
11. b) 12. d) 13. d) 14. b) 15. b) 16. d) 17. c) 18. d) 19. c) 20. b)
21. c) 22. b) 23. c) 24. c) 25. d) 26. c) 27. c) 28. b) 29. a) 30. c)
31. c) 32. c) 33. d) 34. c) 35. b) 36. c) 37. b) 38. c) 39. b) 40. d)
41. a) 42. c) 43. d) 44. b) 45. c) 46. c) 47. d) 48. c) 49. b) 50. c)

Improving the Roads for All

Every good driver wants to share the road with other confident drivers… and this is your chance to help the cause.

Simply by sharing your honest opinion of this book, you'll help new readers prepare for the California DMV Exam and support the improvement of this resource for those to come.

WE WANT YOUR FEEDBACK!

Thank you so much for your support. Best of luck in your exam!

Scan the QR code to leave a review!

CONCLUSION

The main message of this book is crystal clear: Your journey toward becoming a responsible and informed California driver is within reach. The California DMV Exam doesn't have to be an impossible challenge but rather a stepping stone to safer roads and greater freedom.

Throughout these pages, you've gained insights into the rules, techniques, and strategies necessary to navigate the DMV test successfully. You've acquired the knowledge and tools to pass the exam and become a vigilant and courteous driver dedicated to ensuring the safety of yourself and others.

I want to leave you with a success story—that of countless individuals who have diligently studied, applied the principles outlined here, and triumphed on their DMV exam. These individuals now serve as responsible drivers, contributing to the well-being of our communities.

Learning is ongoing even after attaining your driver's license, and staying updated with evolving laws and best practices is essential. Subscribe to the DMV's official newsletter to stay informed and confident in your abilities.

Additionally, consider sharing this valuable resource with friends, family members, or colleagues who may be preparing for their own DMV test. Your support could be instrumental in their success, just as this book has been for you.

Finally, always remember that knowledge is only valuable when put into practice. Apply what you've learned here and remember safe driving isn't just about passing a test; it's a commitment to the well-being of all road users.

Your actions behind the wheel impact not only you but also everyone else sharing the road. So, drive safe, stay informed, and enjoy your journey toward becoming a responsible California driver.

I kindly ask for your review and feedback if you found this book helpful. Your input will help improve this resource for future learners, ensuring their success. Thank you, and here's to your successful journey on the road!

SUPERVISED DRIVING LOG

Learner's Full Name:

_____

Learner's Permit/Provisional License Number:

_____

Supervising Adult's Name:

_____

Date	Start time	End time	Total hours	Location	Conditions (e.g., weather)

Total Supervised Driving Hours:

NOTES

- Ensure that all supervised driving hours are completed in compliance with your state's learner's permit or provisional license requirements.
- Record the start and end times of each driving session accurately.
- Describe the locations/routes driven and any specific conditions, such as weather, encountered during the practice.
- Keep this log in a safe place and update it after each driving session.
- Review and sign the log with the supervising adult to verify the completed hours.

REFERENCES

A Quote from The Perpetual Calendar of Inspiration. Goodreads | Meet Your Next Favorite Book. Accessed October 20, 2023. https://www.goodreads.com/quotes/115553-the-difficulty-in-dealing-with-a-maze-or-labyrinth-lies

California DMV. (n.d.-a). *Auto insurance requirements*. California DMV. Retrieved September 9, 2023, from https://www.dmv.ca.gov/portal/es/vehicle-registration/insurance-requirements/

California DMV. (n.d.-b). *Driver's licenses*. California DMV. https://www.dmv.ca.gov/portal/driver-licenses-identification-cards/driver-licenses-dl/

California DMV. (n.d.-c). *Insurance requirements for vehicle registration*. California DMV. Retrieved September 9, 2023, from https://www.dmv.ca.gov/portal/es/driver-education-and-safety/educational-materials/fast-facts/financial-responsibility-insurance-requirements-for-vehicle-registration-ffvr-18/

California DMV. (n.d.-d). *Provisional licensing*. California DMV. https://www.dmv.ca.gov/portal/driver-education-and-safety/educational-materials/fast-facts/provisional-licensing-ffdl-19/

California DMV. (n.d.-e). *Section 7: Laws and rules of the road (continued)*. California DMV. Retrieved September 9, 2023, from https://www.dmv.ca.gov/portal/es/handbook/california-driver-handbook/laws-and-rules-of-the-road-cont1/

California DMV. (n.d.-f). *Section 8: safe driving (continued)*. California DMV. Retrieved September 9, 2023, from https://www.dmv.ca.gov/portal/es/handbook/california-driver-handbook/safe-driving-cont2/

California DMV. (n.d.-g). *Section 10: financial responsibility, insurance requirements, and collisions*. California DMV. Retrieved September 9, 2023, from https://www.dmv.ca.gov/portal/es/handbook/california-driver-handbook/financial-responsibility-insurance-requirements-and-collisions/

California DMV. (n.d.-h). *Section 10: school buses*. California DMV. Retrieved September 9, 2023, from https://www.dmv.ca.gov/portal/handbook/commercial-driver-handbook/section-10-school-buses/

California DMV. (n.d.-i). *Simple auto insurance*. California DMV. https://www.dmv.ca.gov/portal/business-partner/simple-auto-insurance/

California DMV. (n.d.-j). *Vision impairment and DMV requirements*. California DMV. https://www.dmv.ca.gov/portal/es/driver-education-and-safety/medical-conditions-and-driving/vision-conditions/

California DMV. (2020). *California parent-teen training guide*. https://www.dmv.ca.gov/portal/uploads/2020/06/dl603_compressed.pdf

Coastline Academy. (2021). *Coastline Academy*. Coastlineacademy.com. https://coastlineacademy.com/article/steps-to-get-california-drivers-license

Cook, K. (2023). *Man frees more than 20 drivers stuck on icy Portland off-ramp during storm.*

KGW8. https://www.kgw.com/article/weather/severe-weather/portland-snow good-samaritan-frees-stranded-vehicles/283-9a9f28a9-b58a-48f2-a35a-29d16f179c5f

Faircloth, R. (2023). *"I take full responsibility": DFL state rep. Dan Wolgamott apologizes for recent DWI arrest.* Star Tribune. https://www.startribune.com/i-take-full-responsibility-dfl-state-rep-dan-wolgamott-apologizes-for-recent-dwi-arrest/600291121/?refresh=true

Greenshield. (2019, January 23). *Breathing techniques for anxiety.* Tranquility. https://www.tranquility.app/blog/breathing-techniques

How to get your California drivers license. (n.d.) Driversed.com. https://driversed.com/california/drivers-ed/how-to-get-drivers-license/

Kraut Law Group. (n.d.). *What constitutes impaired driving in California?* Los Angeles Criminal Lawyer. https://www.losangelescriminallawyer.pro/what-constitutes-impaired-driving-in-california.html

Martinez, M. (2022, May 10). *California road signs - everything you should know.* Drive-Safely.net. https://www.drive-safely.net/california-road-signs/

Ounce of prevention, pound of cure. (2012, October 9). University of Cambridge. https://www.cam.ac.uk/research/news/ounce-of-prevention-pound-of-cure

Powell, C. (n.d.). *Colin Powell quotes.* BrainyQuote. https://www.brainyquote.com/quotes/colin_powell_385927

Ramos, N. (2023, June 27). *Ethanol (EtOH) abuse: 6 facts about its dangerous effects.* GateHouse Treatment. https://www.gatehousetreatment.com/blog/ethanol-etoh-abuse/

Ryder. (2022, March 25). *The ultimate guide to getting a driver's license in California.* Skip. https://helloskip.com/blog/the-ultimate-guide-to-getting-a-drivers-license-in-california

Samuel, S., Yahoodik, S., Yamani, Y., Valluru, K., & Fisher, D. L. (2020). Ethical decision making behind the wheel—A driving simulator study. *Transportation Research Interdisciplinary Perspectives, 5,* 100147. https://doi.org/10.1016/j.trip.2020.100147

Trackside classroom. (2017). NNJR. https://nnjr-pca.com/wp-content/uploads/2017/10/Trail-Braking_VIR-Trackside-Classroom.pdf

IMAGE REFERENCES

Alexandre Boucher (2018) *Hombre sosteniendo un teléfono inteligente negro.* [Image]. Unsplash. https://unsplash.com/es/fotos/BNrlDv8w07Y

Clker-Free-Vector-Images (2012). *Fusionando, Tráfico y Señales.* [Image]. Pixabay. https://pixabay.com/es/vectors/fusionando-tráfico-señales-39400/

Clker-Free-Vector-Images (2012). *Señal de tráfico, Cartel de la calle y Signo de curva.* [Image]. Pixabay. https://pixabay.com/es/vectors/señal-de-tráfico-cartel-de-la-calle-26521/

Clker-Free-Vector-Images (2012). *Escuela, Niños y Cruce.* [Image]. Pixabay. https://pixabay.com/es/vectors/escuela-niños-cruce-la-seguridad-32616/

Clker-Free-Vector-Images (2012). *Conducir, La carretera y Producir.* [Image]. Pixabay. https://pixabay.com/es/vectors/conducir-la-carretera-producir-44422/

Clker-Free-Vector-Images (2012). *Girar, Prohibido y Sin turno.* [Image]. Pixabay. https://pixabay.com/es/vectors/girar-prohibido-sin-turno-conducir-44321/

Clker-Free-Vector-Images (2012). *Conducir, Coche y Adelante.* [Image]. Pixabay. https://pixabay.com/es/vectors/conducir-coche-adelante-información-44346/

Clker-Free-Vector-Images (2012). *Conducir, Construcción y La carretera.* [Image]. Pixabay. https://pixabay.com/es/vectors/conducir-construcción-la-carretera-44438/

Clker-Free-Vector-Images (2014). *Gasolinera, Azul y Estación de servicio.* [Image]. Pixabay. https://pixabay.com/es/vectors/gasolinera-azul-estación-de-servicio-296598/

CopyrightFreePictures (2011). *Señal de tráfico, Señales de tráfico y Firmar.* [Image]. Pixabay. https://pixabay.com/es/illustrations/señal-de-tráfico-señales-de-tráfico-6682/

Eugene (2019). *Dos personas en coche en carretera mojada en día lluvioso.* [Image]. Unsplash. https://unsplash.com/es/fotos/J1MHyxAB-UY

Geralt (2020). *Termómetro, Natureleza y Natiuraleza.* [Image]. Pixabay. https://pixabay.com/es/illustrations/termómetro-el-verano-caliente-calor-4767443/

Giorgio Trovato (2020) *Sedán blanco en la carretera cubierta de nieve durante el día.* [Image]. Unsplash. https://unsplash.com/es/fotos/7PUrk4B18tY

James Coleman (2019). *Señalización de la calle roja en la fotografía de enfoque.* [Image]. Unsplash. https://unsplash.com/es/fotos/olN6qebJ3Q0

Joshua Joehne (2018). *Señal de límite de velocidad 25.* [Image]. Unsplash. https://unsplash.com/es/fotos/U4rGvsvop-s

JESHOOTS-com (2018). *Computadora portátil, Mujer y Educación.* [Image]. Pixabay. https://pixabay.com/es/photos/computadora-portátil-mujer-educación-3087585/

Kelly Sikkema (2021). *Palmera verde bajo el cielo blanco durante el día.* [Image]. Unsplash. https://unsplash.com/es/fotos/ek600QSNDag

Kyle Glenn (2018). *White and red do not enter signage* [Image]. Unsplash. https://unsplash.com/photos/dGk-qYBk4OA

Matt Hoffman (2019). *Fotografía de primer plano de carretera mojada.* [Image]. Unsplash. https://unsplash.com/es/fotos/MQjJHTT-diQ

Michael Vi (n.d.). *Freeway 280 entrance sign, turned off ramp meter sign, pedestrian crossing sign next to freeway on ramp.* [Image]. Dreamstime. https://www.dreamstime.com/freeway-entrance-sign-turned-off-ramp-meter-pedestrian-crossing-next-to-image224910524

Momentmal (2017). *Railroad crossing escudo, Tren y Ferrocarril.* [Image]. Pixabay. https://pixabay.com/es/photos/railroad-crossing-escudo-tren-2444337/

Nguyen Dang Hoang Nhu (2020). *Persona escribiendo en papel blanco.* [Image]. Unsplash. https://unsplash.com/es/fotos/qDgTQOYk6B8

OpenClipart-Vectors (2013). *Tráfico de doble sentido, Camino de dos vía y Tráfico opuesto.* [Image]. Pixabay. https://pixabay.com/es/vectors/tráfico-de-doble-sentido-148887/

OpenClipart-Vectors (2013). *No hay vehículos de motor, Hay motos y Señal de tráfico.* [Image]. Pixabay. https://pixabay.com/es/vectors/no-hay-vehículos-de-motor-hay-motos-160698/

OpenClipart-Vectors (2013). *Ningún giro a la izquierda, Señal de tráfico y Firmar.* [Image]. Pixabay. https://pixabay.com/es/vectors/ningún-giro-a-la-izquierda-160689/

OpenClipart-Vectors (2013). *Tráfico, Firmar y Detener.* [Image]. Pixabay. https://pixabay.com/es/vectors/tráfico-firmar-detener-157617/

Peter Kalonji (2020). *Una vista brumosa del puente Golden Gate.* [Image]. Unsplash. https://unsplash.com/es/fotos/fp1JayQP6IU

Sebastian Enrique (2023). *Una carretera llena de mucho tráfico debajo de un puente.* [Image]. Unsplash. https://unsplash.com/es/fotos/fITjgoVw6GU

Stephan Lehner (2019). *Mujeres caminando en el carril peatonal.* [Image]. Unsplash. https://unsplash.com/es/fotos/zLPivr_4ma0

TheMilMarZone (2022). *No u turn, Señal de tráfico y Cartel de la calle.* [Image]. Pixabay. https://pixabay.com/es/illustrations/no-u-turn-señal-de-tráfico-7133041/

Tim Samuel (2020). *Reflejo De La Carretera De La Ciudad En El Espejo Lateral.* [Image]. Pexels. https://www.pexels.com/es-es/foto/reflejo-de-la-carretera-de-la-ciudad-en-el-espejo-lateral-5835336/

Tungsten Rising (2022). *Una señal amarilla de cruce peatonal sentada al costado de una carretera.* [Image]. Unsplash. https://unsplash.com/es/fotos/Ne4ufJjVfHU

Wikimediaimages (2015). *Señal de tráfico, Ruso y Prohibido.* [Image]. Pixabay. https://pixabay.com/es/vectors/señal-de-tráfico-ruso-prohibido-867215/

Will Porada (2019). *Detener la señalización.* [Image]. Unsplash. https://unsplash.com/es/fotos/ZaGcU6BxJEc

Kindel Media (2021). *Hombre calle escritura sujetando.* [Image]. Pexels. https://www.pexels.com/es-es/foto/hombre-calle-escritura-sujetando-7715248/s/foto/hombre-calle-escritura-sujetando-7715248/

Velocidad, limitado, 35 señal de tráfico, calle, letrero, autopista, viajes, transporte,tráfico, símbolo (n.d.). [Image]. Pxfuel. https://www.pxfuel.com/es/free-photo-jqxqq

Fongbeerredhot (n.d.). *Persona que empuja el claxon mientras conduce sentado de uncoche de prensa de volante, sonido de bocina para advertir a otras personas enconcepto de tráfico.* [Image]. Freepik. https://www.freepik.es/fotos-premium/persona-que-empuja-claxon-mientras-conduce-sentado-coche-prensa-volante-sonido-bocina-advertir-otras-personas-concepto-trafico_21015364.htm

OpenClipart-vectors (2013). *Imagen de Señal de tráfico, Firmar y Señales de tráfico.*[Image]. Pixabay. https://pixabay.com/es/vectors/señal-de-tráfico-firmar-160660/

DOWNLOADABLE FLASHCARDS
AND AUDIO FILES

If the QR codes don't work, email us at drivesafelypublising@
yahoo.com

Flashcards California DMV Handbook

Audio Files DMV Handbook